THE GARDENER'S PALETTE

Creating Color in the Garden

~

SYDNEY EDDISON

PHOTOGRAPHY BY STEVE SILK

Contemporary Books

Chicago   New York   San Francisco   Lisbon   London   Madrid   Mexico City
Milan   New Delhi   San Juan   Seoul   Singapore   Sydney   Toronto

Library of Congress Cataloging-in-Publication Data

Eddison, Sydney, 1932–.
    The gardener's palette: exploring color in the garden / Sydney
Eddison; Photography by Steve Silk.
        p.   cm.
    ISBN 0-8092-9893-7
    1. Color in gardening.   I. Title.

SB454.3.C64 E33   2002
635.9'68—dc21   2001047691

Contemporary Books

A Division of The **McGraw·Hill** *Companies*

1 2 3 4 5 6 7 8 9 0   SSI/SSI   1 0 9 8 7 6 5 4 3 2

ISBN 0-8092-9893-7

All photographs by Steve Silk except the following pages: 6 by Lee Anne White; 20 (left, center) by Sydney Eddison; 28 and 29 (2) by Ragna Goddard; 40, J. M. W. Turner, *The Burning of the Houses of Lords and Commons*, courtesy of the Philadelphia Museum of Art: The John Howard McFadden Collection; 44, Claude Monet, *Garden at Sainte-Adresse*, courtesy of The Metropolitan Museum of Art, purchased with special contributions and purchase funds given or bequeathed by friends of the Museum, 1967 (67.241). Photograph © 1989 The Metropolitan Museum of Art; 47, Claude Monet, *The Artist's Garden at Giverny*, courtesy of the Yale University Art Gallery, collection of Mr. and Mrs. Paul Mellon, B.A. 1929; 49, Vincent Van Gogh, *Self Portrait with a Straw Hat*, courtesy of The Metropolitan Museum of Art, bequest of Miss Adalaide Milton deGroot (1876–1967). Photograph © 1982 The Metropolitan Museum of Art; 41 (top), 59 (bottom left), and 66 by Sydney Eddison; 80, Vincent Van Gogh, *Night Café (le café de nuit)*, courtesy of the Yale University Art Gallery, bequest of Stephen Carlton Clark, B.A. 1903; 102 by Lee Anne White; 105, 108, 114, 118 (bottom), 119, 147 (2), 148 (top), 157, and 180 by Sydney Eddison; 181 by Lee Anne White; 186 by Ragna Goddard; 190 by Sydney Eddison; 199 by John Longstreth; 218, Paul Gauguin, *Parau Parau* (Whispered Words), courtesy of the Yale University Art Gallery, John Hay Whitney, B.A. 1926, M.A. (Hon.) 1956, collection; 221 by Lee Anne White

McGraw-Hill books are available at special quantity discounts to use as premiums and sales promotions, or for use in corporate training programs. For more information, please write to the Director of Special Sales, Professional Publishing, McGraw-Hill, Two Penn Plaza, New York, NY 10121-2298. Or contact your local bookstore.

For my niece, Jeni Webber, with love

~

To
Betsy,

with all good wishes —

Sydney Eddison

CONTENTS

FOREWORD BY PAMELA J. HARPER   ix

ACKNOWLEDGMENTS   xiii

INTRODUCTION   xvii

1. REDISCOVERING THE COLOR WHEEL
Color Theory in Brief   1

2. THE VOCABULARY OF COLOR
Speaking a Common Language   13

3. NATURE AND ART
Looking at Color   39

4. HARMONY AND CONTRAST
How Color Schemes Work   61

5. GARDEN COLOR SCHEMES
Thematic Gardens   73

6. FROM COLLAGE TO CONTAINERS
Experimenting with Color   91

7. ANNUALS AND TENDER PERENNIALS
FOR CONTAINERS
Choosing the Best   107

8. APPEARANCES
The Way We See Colors in the Garden   121

9. NATURE'S CHOICE
The Benign Influence of Green   131

10. GRAY
The Good Neighbor   145

11. WHITE
Star Quality   159

12. BACKGROUND COLORS
They Also Serve Who Only Stand and Wait   171

13. CHOICES
Limiting the Means   183

14. THE MAGIC NUMBER THREE
Another Way to Limit the Means   203

15. BORROWING COLOR SCHEMES
The Sincerest Form of Flattery   217

THE LAST WORD   231

FOREWORD

Who better than Sydney Eddison to simplify for others the complex subject of garden color? An experienced teacher and eloquent writer, she makes lucid the often arcane language of color. In the manner of friend talking to friend—confident yet never dictatorial or patronizing—she shares not only what she has learned, but also the excitement of learning and the joy in her chosen way of life.

In this survey of the multifaceted subject of garden color, the author marries the study of color across such diverse disciplines as stage lighting, painting, and fabric design. Her life experience, combined with an extensive knowledge of plants and many years of trial and error in her own acclaimed garden, has enabled her to take gardeners far beyond the basics.

The book, says its author, is about learning to look. But it is also about learning to pay heed to one's feelings and to notice how, as in color therapy and art, color in the garden can be used to manipulate emotions—to enliven, sedate, or surprise. *The Gardener's Palette* encourages exploration and experimentation. Once aware of the serenity evoked by gentle pinks, blues, and lavenders versus the exuberance of "hot" scarlet, orange, and warm yellow, gardeners usually prefer one or the other. Yet, such preferences need not limit the colors used. Vivid scarlets, oranges, and warm yellows become mellow when reduced to pastels. And a single dab of complementary red makes vibrant an otherwise peaceful green scene.

Although staying with analogous colors all but guarantees harmony, Eddison points out that contrasting schemes can also be harmonized by employing one or more of nature's basic colors of green, gray, brown, and buffs, along with subdued foliage tones.

Many different aspects of color are discussed in bite-sized, digestible chapters that include such subjects as the preeminence of green; the value of gray for reconciling differences in hue, value, or intensity; why subtle color associations are often best appreciated in containers; and how—given sufficient space—such unsympathetic adjacent pairs as crimson and scarlet can be rendered compatible in incremental progressions.

Nothing is overlooked, from how colors are influenced by time of day and season of the year to the effect of regional surroundings and the role of texture, size, and shape of the flower.

The color-cowardly will be helped and heartened by this unique book. Even experienced gardeners, artists, and the color-courageous, who prefer to work things out by eye and instinct, will find abundant tips and suggestions for unusual garden and container combinations. *The Gardener's Palette* is a book that will seldom stay unopened.

~

PAMELA J. HARPER

Author of *Perennials: How to Select, Grow, and Enjoy* and
Time-Tested Plants: Thirty Years in a Four-Season Garden

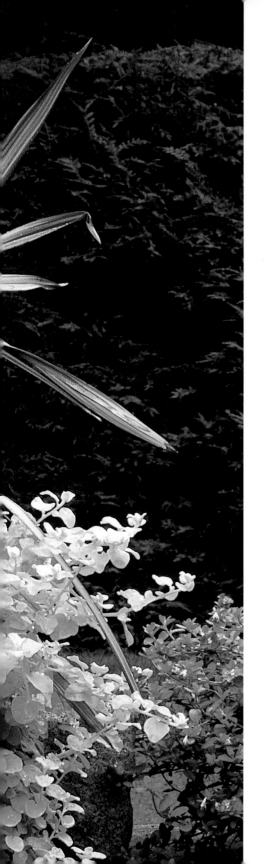

ACKNOWLEDGMENTS

SYDNEY'S: The romantic notion of a writer struggling in solitude with the muse, is hardly accurate in my case. My struggles with the complex subject of color have been inflicted on numerous friends, acquaintances, and associates, to say nothing of my long-suffering husband. For his and their forbearance, I am deeply grateful.

No writer is an island, and many people have contributed to the creation of this book, most importantly my partner, photographer Steve Silk, with whom I had already worked on several stories for *Fine Gardening* magazine. This brings me to another debt of gratitude: for kindly allowing us the use of images that first appeared in the magazine, we would like to thank Suzanne Roman and editors Lee Anne White and Todd Meier.

Local businesses, Hollandia Nurseries, Lexington Gardens, and Burr Farm Garden Center have been generous in permitting us to take photographs and even borrow plants, for which I am grateful.

It goes without saying that our greatest debt is to the wonderful gardeners who have so effectively employed nature's glorious palette. These garden artists have made this book possible.

I am personally indebted to the following talented friends: lighting designer Marilyn Renegal, who refreshed my memory about the behavior of colored light and its power in the theater; Betty Ajay, a landscape designer and friend of many years, with whom I have kept up a running dialogue about color and design since the 1980s; another longtime friend, Gregory Piotrowski, formerly a gardener at the New York Botanical Garden, who reviewed the manuscript with regard to botanical nomenclature; Pamela Harper, whom I came to know through her lectures and books and who has always been a source of inspiration; and newer gardening friends, Betty Grindrod and Gay Vincent-Canal, who spent time talking to me about color and sharing their insights and professional knowledge.

The labor of making an unwieldy manuscript into a book fell to my editor, Anne Knudsen, who guided me through reducing its length to manageable proportions. She also suggested the title, *The Gardener's Palette: Exploring Color in the Garden*, which perfectly expressed my intention. My agent Jane Dystel, who has been behind the book from the start, provided support throughout, and the admirable Kathy Dennis has ironed out bumps in the road to production. I feel fortunate to have had this team on my side.

STEVE'S: Without *Fine Gardening* magazine, this book might never have happened. The magazine introduced me to the delights of photographing gardens and to Sydney Eddison, who graciously invited me to accompany her on the trip across the rainbow that led to publication of this book. I am also indebted to my wife, Kate Emery, my partner in life and in the garden, for her patience with my passion for chasing the light. And thanks to my son David, who as a two-year-old accompanied me on many photo outings and now thinks every house in the world has a beautiful garden in the backyard. If only he were right.

Finally, I owe a debt of gratitude to the many gardeners who welcomed me into their gardens, dawn or dusk. Without their ephemeral creations, the photographs in this book would not have been possible. These fine gardeners include: Betty Ajay, Bethel, CT; The Bellevue (WA) Botanical Garden; Helen Bodian, Millerton, NY; Nancy Britz, Hamilton, MA; Martine and Richard Copeland, Roxbury, CT; Chrissie D'Esopo, Avon, CT; Elizabeth Park, Hartford, CT; Jerry Fritz, Bedminster, PA; Garden of Ideas, Joseph Keller, Ridgefield, CT; Judy Glattstein, Frenchtown, NJ; Raymond Hagel, Westport, CT; Danny Hills, Portland, OR; Hillstead Museum, Farmington, CT; Hollandia Nursery, Newtown, CT; Institute for Ecosystem Studies, Millbrook, NY; Gary Keim, Swarthmore, PA; Verle Lessig, Chicago, IL; Ruth and Jim Levitan, Stamford, CT; Logee's Greenhouses, Danielson, CT; Longwood Gardens, Kennett Square, PA; Lynden Miller, Sharon, CT; Pat and John Miszuk, Newtown, CT; Marcella and Glen Moore, Eugene, OR; Richard, Dorethy, and Oona Mulligan, Newtown, CT; Munich Botanic Garden, Munich, Germany; New York Botanic Garden, New York, NY; Marietta and Ernie O'Byrne, Eugene, OR; Betty Ravenholt, Seattle, WA; Wesley Rouse, Southbury, CT; Mary Stambaugh, Newtown, CT; Elisabeth Sheldon, Lansing, NY; Smith Botanic Garden, Northampton, MA; Staudensichtungsgarten, Freising, Germany; Steepleview Gardens, Kathy Loomis, Colebrook, CT; Ken Twombly, Twombly Nursery, Monroe, CT; Georgia Vance, Mount Solon, VA; Westpark, Munich, Germany; White Flower Farm, Litchfield, CT; Peter Wooster, Roxbury, CT.

INTRODUCTION

Learning to Look

IN A LONG GARDENING LIFE, nothing has given me more pleasure than playing with color schemes in flower beds and containers. Hence, *The Gardener's Palette*.

While color is an extremely complex phenomenon, I don't think gardeners need to know everything there is to know about it in order to put together attractive garden combinations. Of all the books I have now read on the subject, *Color in Your Garden*, by Penelope Hobhouse, is still the best. But like color itself, the book is extremely complex. I hope this book makes it a little bit easier.

My improbable credentials for attempting to simplify color for gardeners are a degree in theater, which I taught for twenty years; the modest skills of a Sunday painter; and a beloved garden that has been my palette, my textbook, and the joy of my life.

Before I began to write, I felt obliged to find out as much as I could about color. In the course of my research, I learned amazing things about the way colors behave. And my excursions into the world of color vision were intellectually stimulating. But many of my discoveries didn't seem to apply to arranging colors in the garden.

Gardeners don't need to fathom the mysteries of light and vision. Instead, they need to acquire a nodding acquaintance with simple color theory and to familiarize themselves with the color wheel. Most of all, they need to trust their own instincts and learn to look.

When I was a theater student, I studied stage lighting and was surprised to find out that colored light does not behave like the pigment in paints. With paints, you can mix all other colors from red, yellow, and blue, the so-called primary colors. If you combine red and yellow, you get orange. Blue and red make purple, and blue and yellow, green. But the light primaries are different. Instead of red, yellow, and blue, they are red, blue, and green. I had no trouble with red and blue light making magenta or the mixture of blue and green resulting in a color called "cyan." But it affronted my painter's common sense to discover that, mixed together, red light and green light make yellow light. As soon as possible, I gave up lighting in favor of scene painting, which *did* make sense to me, and was more fun.

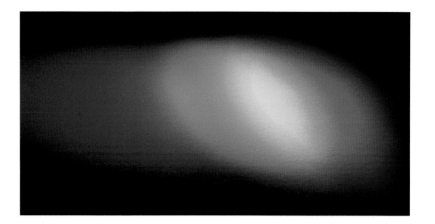

It wasn't until I began doing research for this book that I returned to the subject of light. It can't be avoided because all color theories are based on Sir Isaac Newton's discoveries about light.

In 1666, the great physicist, then a twenty-three-year-old instructor at Cambridge University, in England, proved that white light contains all the colors of the rainbow. His experiments involved intercepting beams of sunlight with a glass prism. The prism split the white light into bands of its respective colors: red, orange, yellow, green, blue, and violet.

It was a logical step from the arc of the rainbow to the circular diagram that Newton devised to illustrate relationships between the colors, which always appear in the same order. As he was concerned with light, not pigment, an annotated black-and-white drawing served his purpose.

It wasn't until 100 years later that British engraver Moses Harris, whom you will meet in Chapter 1, published the first full-color diagram of a color wheel. He observed a natural progression of colors that "gave the hint that they should be placed in a circular form."

The significance of Harris's color wheel for artists and engravers was that they could see at a glance how the colors are related to each other: red next to its offspring, orange, and orange next to its other parent, yellow, and so on. This logical arrangement of colors has value for gardeners, too. In the garden, understanding color relationships is the key to success.

Understanding light is not important for gardeners. Although light determines how we see colors in the garden, it is something over which we have no control. We are stuck with the light we get. But as you will see, we can control our use of color.

Chambers Twentieth Century Dictionary tells us that color is "a property whereby bodies have different appearances to the eye through surface reflection or absorption of rays." But for gardeners, it is more important to know what a color *looks* like than what it is. We are a simple lot. Even if we know that a red rose only appears red because its surface reflects that wavelength of colored light, we accept its redness. If it *looks* red, it *is* red, because in the garden, it is the eye of the beholder that counts.

In sifting through the research of two years and thinking about what gardeners need to know about color, I kept coming back to painting and painters. Painters don't necessarily know anything about the science of color. It is what they *see* that makes them what they are, not what they know. That's when I began to feel I was on the right track.

Color in the garden is about looking and seeing. One of the great daylily hybridizers of the last 100 years was an uneducated rice picker from Louisiana. Edna Spalding didn't know anything about color theory, but she knew a muddy-looking pink daylily when she saw it. What she had was a discriminating eye and absolute integrity. If a daylily wasn't a pure enough pink, onto the compost pile it went.

On the surface of it, Spalding doesn't have much in common with artists like Claude Monet, Vincent van Gogh, J. M. W. Turner, Paul Gauguin, and other great colorists. But she knew how to look, and so did they. That's what it takes to put colors together effectively in a painting and a garden.

Looking is nothing more than the conscious act of paying attention. You have to look at colors carefully enough to recognize their unique qualities. Then, you have to compare them to one another and see how they are related.

For better or for worse, this is the tack I've taken in *The Gardener's Palette*. During the course of writing the book, I researched colors, experimented with colors, fretted over colors. But most important of all, I learned to *see* colors. Looking is the first step; *seeing* comes with understanding. In *The Gardener's Palette*, I share with you all I have seen. The book is based on the practical experience of putting colors together in the garden. This is what I love most, do best, and have been doing for forty years.

~

SYDNEY EDDISON

REDISCOVERING THE COLOR WHEEL

Color Theory in Brief

I BOUGHT MY FIRST COLOR WHEEL following an invitation to speak at a meeting of the North American Rock Garden Society. Being a perennial gardener who had never aspired to growing temperamental plants from the heights, I wasn't sure what I could offer. Then, the idea came to me to show slides of color schemes using alpines. My cospeaker would talk about the plants, and I would talk about color. I began doing my homework. That's when I discovered *Color in Your Garden*, by Penelope Hobhouse.

Color in Your Garden is not an easy read—the text is dense, thorough, and scholarly. Yet, it is fascinating, particularly the chapter on the nature of color. A picture of the color wheel rang a bell, and on the strength of it, I went in search of one. Color wheels cost about $6 and are available at any art store. I will always be grateful to Hobhouse for reintroducing me to this delightful interactive toy. After playing with it for a few days and taking it out into the garden, I decided that basically everything a gardener needs to know about color is explained right on the color wheel.

I used it to illustrate color relationships for the rock gardeners and to show them why certain combinations work well together. Although the program was warmly received, I knew that the audience would much rather have seen slides of minute plants clinging gamely to mountainsides. Rock gardeners simply don't care much about color. However, the talk inspired me to pursue the subject further and launched my speaking career.

A SIMPLE TOOL TO PLAN COLOR

~

In a way, the color wheel changed my life. For years, I had been perfectly happy combining colors in the garden by guess and by God and by eye. But with the color wheel, I began to *plan* color schemes. Having no room in the garden to try them, I resorted to containers. You will see evidence throughout this book that container gardening has become my latest passion, thanks to the color wheel.

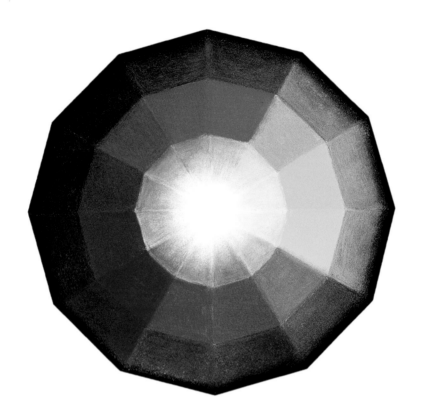

What makes a color wheel so useful is that it shows you how the colors are related to each other by their positions around the circle. All you have to do is look at the arrangement of colors. Red-orange is between red and orange. And why not? Red-orange is the child of red and orange.

Although it is a huge over-simplification to say that there are only two approaches to combining colors in the garden, it is substantially true. You can either go with the flow and use the colors that are next to each other on the color wheel, in which case you will arrive at harmony. Or you can cause a bit of a stir by putting together colors that have nothing in common, thereby creating contrast. But to do either well, you need to know where all the colors belong in the first place.

With a color wheel, it is easy to see that there is a family like-ness between red, red-orange, and orange. Moving on, yellow-orange lies between its parents, yellow and orange, and resembles both. The rest of the colors continue around the circle in this logi-cal fashion: red, red-orange, orange, yellow-orange, yellow, yellow-green, green, and so on. As the color wheel is based on the rainbow, the order of the colors is the same: red, orange, yellow, green, blue, and violet.

The text on the color wheel tells you that adjacent colors are *analogous*, that is, alike in some respects. But you already know that from looking. Each color has pigment in common with the colors on either side of it. Therefore, analogous colors are the stuff of harmony.

Colors lying directly opposite each other are described as *complementary*. Complementary colors have nothing in common and are as remote from each other as two colors can get. Putting them together results in a dramatic contrast. Essentially, this is all the color theory you need to know: most effective color schemes are based either on contrast or on harmony.

Harmonies and Contrasts

With my rediscovery of the color wheel, I began to notice examples of contrast and harmony everywhere. Closely related colors account for much of the appeal of Liberty prints and Martha Stewart's coordinated line of interior paints. Color harmonies are the way to achieve what Stewart describes in her ads for the line as "a serene and cohesive interior."

Contrasts have the opposite effect. They are staples of the marketplace and jump out at you from posters, calendars, magazine covers, and book jackets. Greeting card designers owe a significant debt to complementary pairs like red and green, yellow and violet.

Color and Art

Playing with the color wheel brought me back to the art world again. I began to look for examples of contrast and harmony in paintings. And the search made museum visits doubly interesting. I used to take the color wheel with me on these excursions. It never ceased to amaze me how often painters used complements or a series of related colors or, indeed, both. Meanwhile, I started taking pictures of my own garden and others to show examples of contrast and harmony in the garden. Then came the addition of slides from museum trips to illustrate the same contrasts and harmonies in paintings.

One thing led to another, and in 1996, I began teaching a workshop called "Color Theory Made Practical," at the Institute of Ecosystem Studies, in Millbrook, New York. Students were provided with color wheels and allowed to pick leaves and flower heads from the perennial gardens to create contrasts and harmonies. In winter, we used paint chips, colored paper, and old garden catalogs instead.

My love of art and my good fortune in meeting painters, photographers, designers, and graphic artists who have turned to gardening, either as a profession or a pastime, led me to realize that success with color has less to do with artistic training than with a capacity for *looking*. When artistic people look at colors, they are able to see subtle likenesses and differences between them. I also realized that the ability to look at colors is a skill that can be acquired.

Anyone can learn to look. And one of the best ways to start is by studying the color wheel and comparing each color to its rela-

A GARLAND OF COLOR

This enchanting wreath is a most unusual color wheel, a rainbow of flowers. Forgive me for digressing briefly to introduce the designer, my niece, Jeni Webber. Jeni started out as a painter, switched to horticulture, and is now a landscape architect in Berkeley, California.

Jeni loves color as much as her aunt. In graduate school, she studied color theory, but that was a few years ago. This is what she has to say about it today. "You learn the rules. Then, you try to break them. You push the envelope, but you realize that some things really don't work. For instance, it's true that blue and violet rarely look good together. I tried it just the other day and had to dig it out."

Spoken like a real gardener! This niece of mine is a free spirit. She'll try anything. She loves purple and chartreuse, red and pink, purple and red, orange and purple. She also loves what she does because it gives her a chance to experiment with so many different plants and color schemes.

Jeni and I see eye to eye about color, gardens, and people. When I asked her to make me a color wheel out of real flowers and leaves, she obliged with the beautiful wreath that you see here.

When she began working on the floral color wreath, Jeni found the biggest challenge was to choose from among the hundreds of colors in the garden and to arrange them to reflect the hues on the color wheel. But once she got started, her eye took over.

"You just see that this red has a little coral in it and should go on the orange side, not the side with violet in it. From the red-orange to the red-violet was the most fun to work on, though the purples were exciting, too. There are so many gradations. And some have more red in them than others. But once you have all of one color together, you definitely see that this purple is going toward red, and that one, toward blue. The only way to do it is to assemble a lot of colors and spread them all out. Until you have plenty to choose from, it's hard to make comparisons."

tions, near and far. You will soon begin to see likenesses between adjacent colors and notice differences between those that are farther apart. Right away, you will be struck by the extreme difference between colors that are directly opposite each other on the color wheel. These are the complementaries: red and green; red-violet and yellow-green; violet and yellow; blue-violet and yellow-orange; and so forth around the circle.

COLORS ON THE WHEEL AND IN THE GARDEN

There are only twelve colors on the color wheel, so making comparisons among them is relatively easy. But out in the garden, there are many, many more colors. Figuring out where they all belong is the trick.

Man and nature have certainly conspired to produce a vast number of colors. The first explosion of man-made color began in the nineteenth century with scientists like English chemist William Henry Perkins. Perkins stumbled on the color we call mauve by mistake. In 1856, he was trying to synthesize the drug quinine from coal tar, but instead, came up with a purple dye.

Today, we are faced with an embarrassment of riches. Scientists are always finding ways of making new colors. And computer technology offers the possibility of literally millions more. Not to be outdone, plant hybridizers are on a roll. Daylilies, chrysanthemums, dahlias, peonies, pansies, daffodils, roses, and bearded irises now come in dozens of previously unheard of colors. And the end is nowhere in sight.

No wonder we need a color wheel! Somewhere in that circle, all the colors—new and old—have a logical place. To find it, you have to study each color in relation to those most like it and, using the color wheel, figure out whether a red belongs on the orange side or the violet side.

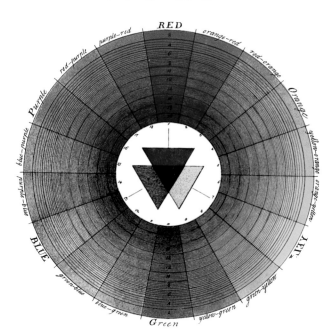

THE HARRIS COLOR WHEEL

When Moses Harris published the first pigment-based color wheel in 1766, in his treatise, *The Natural System of Colours*, he explained that he had "endeavored to take nature for his guide." Although he could only approximate the seamless progression of colors in nature's rainbow, he succeeded in creating a color wheel of great refinement. His colors blend so gradually from one to another that you can see each one progressively assuming the character of the next.

Almost imperceptibly, red begins to lose itself in orange. Orange leaves its redness behind in stages as it melts into yellow. Yellow's sunny nature gives way first to yellow-green, then green, which gradually yields to blue, and blue to violet.

Finally, violet becomes more and more like red until all trace of blue is subsumed.

Modern color wheels are crude by comparison to the Harris model. The steps between colors are abrupt and clearly marked, but the format remains faithful to the original. As Harris explained, the three primary colors are "the greatest opposites in quality to each other and naturally take their places at the greatest distance from each other in the circle." They are evenly spaced with three colors between them.

The three secondary colors—orange, green, and violet—are evenly spaced between their parents. Harris reasoned that "if red and yellow be mixed together, they will compose an orange; and therefore it is placed between red and yellow. If yellow and blue are mixed together, green is produced and accordingly takes its place between those two colors, and so blue and red producing a purple, the purple must be placed between them."

On either side of the secondary colors are the tertiaries—the colors produced by mixing the two secondary colors. Harris includes twelve intermediate color mixtures, but modern color wheels are confined to three primaries, three secondaries, and six tertiaries.

TODAY'S COLOR WHEELS

~

Of the color wheels available today—and there are several—I have found this one from the Color Wheel Company in Philomath, Ore-

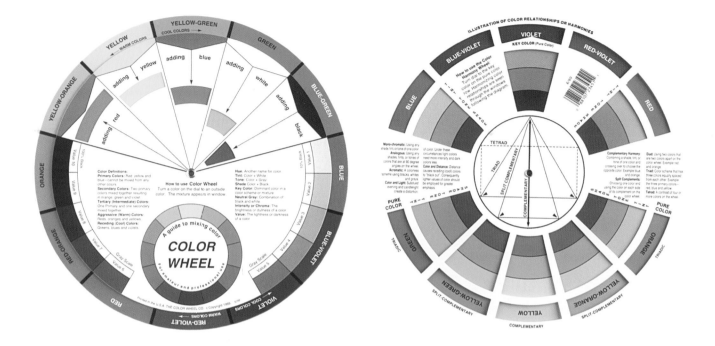

gon to be the most useful. Using it is incredibly easy. The instructions on each side are simple and clear. On one side are the color schemes. Turn the dial to a key color, and its complement shows up in a windowlike opening, along with its color partners in several other possible schemes.

On the other side are definitions of common color terms. There is nothing scientific about the language of color, and there is no standardized vocabulary. The terms are in everyday use, and there is only a handful. That's all a gardener needs.

THE VOCABULARY OF COLOR

Speaking a Common Language

COLOR TERMINOLOGY HAS ALWAYS BEEN more evocative than exact, beginning with Moses Harris. Not much is known about Harris, except that he was an engraver by profession. But his landmark work, *The Natural System of Colours*, laid the foundation for the system that is still in use today.

His color wheel was the first ever printed in full color. And he is reputedly the first individual to organize colors into a logical scheme based on "the dependence they have on each other." In other words, their relationships.

In *The Natural System of Colours*, Harris wrote: "By the word colour, or colours, we would be understood to mean one or all of those appearances which are seen in the rainbow refracted by the prism, or that so beautifully decorate the leaves of flowers."

Harris used common English flowers of field and garden to show what he meant by the terms *red*, *yellow*, and *blue*; *green*, *orange*, and *violet*. And though color science has made giant strides since then, there is still no better way to define colors than to give examples.

So, above are six modern garden plants to represent the primary and secondary colors at full intensity: for red, the dahlia 'Bishop of

THIS PAGE, FROM LEFT: Dahlia, helenium, delphiniums, hosta, California poppies, and purple iris.

OPPOSITE, TOP: Pink is a tint of red.

BOTTOM: These tulips are a very dark shade of red.

Landaff'; yellow, the flowers of *Helenium autumnale* 'Butterpat'; blue, delphiniums; *Hosta* 'Royal Standard,' the quintessence of green; orange, California poppies; and the rich velvety color of certain irises for purple.

FROM COLORS INTO WORDS

There are only two words, *color* and *hue*, to describe the "appearances" illustrated by these plants. But as soon as these clear, intense colors are lightened, darkened, or dulled, they become *tints*, *shades*, and *tones*.

Tints, Shades, and Tones

In painting, a *tint* is any pure color lightened by the addition of white—pink is a tint of red. A color darkened by black is a *shade*—so-called "black tulips" are really a dark shade of red. And a *tone* is any color dulled by the addition of gray. Nature has other methods of creating subdued, neutral versions of pure hues. Most of the dark colors in the foliage of ornamental shrubs and trees, like purple smokebush and the weeping purple beech, are tones.

Nature creates subdued purple tones.

Intensity

Harris divided his color wheel into "twenty parts or degrees of power, from the deepest or strongest to the weakest." In nature, of course, the progression in each hue is infinitely graduated, but modern color wheels show only four "degrees of power": full strength, a tint, a tone, and a shade. The terms used today to describe the relative potency of a color aren't any particular improvement over "power." There are several of them, however. And they all mean the same thing. Take your pick from *intensity*, *purity*, *saturation*, and *chroma*. I use them all, just for variety.

Around the rim of the color wheel are the intense, fully saturated hues represented by the garden flowers on page 14. Within the circle are the tints, tones, and shades of each color, all of which are lower in saturation or intensity than the pure colors.

Value

The lightness or darkness of a color is described by the term *value*. Looking into the face of a Johnny-jump-up, you can see immediately that yellow has a lighter value than purple. In fact, yellow has the lightest value of all the spectral colors. Yellow-green, yellow-orange, and orange are relatively light colors; their opposites, red-violet, blue-violet, and blue, are relatively dark. Red and green fall in the middle of the light-to-dark scale and are of about equal value.

Yellow has the lightest value of all the spectral colors.

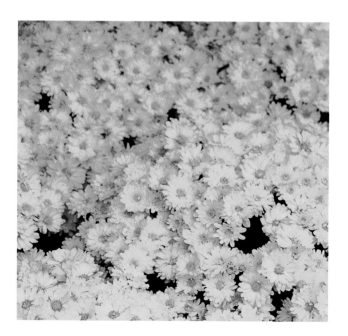

White, gray, and black are without color. *Achromatic* is the technical word. But in terms of value, white is the lightest of all colors, even lighter than yellow; black, the darkest; and in between, the grays run the gamut from almost as light as white to almost as dark as black.

In the plant world, there are few snow-whites and no true blacks, but there are literally thousands of different grays. And Nature does nothing as simple as using gray pigment to create these subtle tones. Her grays are tinted with other colors: the brown-gray of bark, the green-gray of lichen, the pink-gray of maple twigs in winter, and so many more.

White is the lightest of all colors.

Warm and Cool Colors

In addition to tints, tones, and shades and degrees of lightness, darkness, and intensity, there remains one color concept with which everyone is familiar, temperature. Although some experts dispute the existence of color temperature, the meaning of *warm colors* and *cool colors* is clear.

Red, orange, and yellow are the warm colors because they evoke images of the fireplace, golden summer days, and molten sunsets. Warm colors advance toward you, just as heat does, but cool colors withdraw. Green, blue, and violet are the colors of depths and distances—of far-off mountain tops and "the glassy, cool, translucent wave" of John Milton's *Comus*.

Glowing sunsets radiate heat, while haze-wrapped mountains bespeak a cooler atmosphere.

Warm colors can be either cheerful and comforting or passionate, exciting, and even dangerous. Cool colors are just the opposite—soothing, restful, and serene. Being aware of the emotional impact of warm and cool colors can help gardeners choose the kind of garden that is right for them. But there are warm versions and cool versions of every color.

Although red is a warm color, some reds are warmer than others, depending on their composition. Hot reds have orange in them; cool reds, a bit of blue. With the exception of pure, primary red, the reds lean either toward orange or toward blue.

If you study the red geranium in the photograph on the next page and compare it to the color wheel, you can *see* that the color leans more toward its red-orange neighbor than toward its red-violet neighbor. In the peony illustrated, the hint of red-violet is not

obvious until you look at it with the red-violet clematis. Then, you can see the family relationship. And notice how much better the peony looks with its cooler relation, red-violet, than with its warmer relation, red-orange.

All colors exhibit this Janus character, with one face toward the warm side of the spectrum and the other toward the cool. Violet is a cool color, but if it contains enough red, it becomes a warm color. Even blue can be either warm or cool. A blue with violet in it is warmer than a blue with green in it.

Green with blue in it is the coolest green, and yellow-green is warm for green but cool for a yellow. As yellow approaches orange, it gets warmer and warmer and so on around the color circle. We owe this insight to Moses Harris and his carefully graduated color wheel. Although he never referred to color temperature as such, he showed us "The manner in which each Colour is formed, and its Composition."

Some colors clash when warm and cool versions are put side by side, but the greens are all perfectly at home together. The same can't be said of blues. Gertrude Jekyll, that most gifted of English garden

THIS PAGE: The peony in the center looks much better with its cool, red-violet neighbor on the right than it does with its hot, red-orange neighbor on the left.

OPPOSITE: Green has two faces, cool blue-green (TOP LEFT) and warm yellow-green (TOP RIGHT). Yellow can also be warm or cool. The cool daylilies and warmer black-eyed Susans are still not as warm as the yellow-orange dahlia.

designers, always separated true blues from violet-blues. She kept the pure, cool blues of delphiniums at one end of her famous border and the warmer blue-violets and purples of ageratum and asters at the other.

In her masterwork on color, *Colour Schemes for the Flower Garden*, first published in 1908, Jekyll wrote: "I prefer to avoid, except in occasional details, a mixture of blue and purple." Delphinium blue, lovely as it is, presents a problem. Perfect with whites, pinks, and pale yellows, it puts blues with violet in them to shame, making them look dingy by comparison.

It takes practice to develop a good eye for color temperature. And the only way to do it is by making endless comparisons. But

COMPATIBLE COLORS

I began to take more than a passing interest in color temperature early in my gardening career. I made this note in my first garden journal: "Pink *Phlox* 'Dodo Hansbury Forbes' has been lovely for about three weeks and is now going by. But the supposedly wine-red Phlox 'Floreat' is a rather horrid color, a kind of American Beauty red that looks awful with 'Dodo Hansbury Forbes.'"

That was my first inkling that warm pinks and cool pinks, like warm reds and cool reds, are incompatible. This suspicion was confirmed later when I planted a peony called 'Coral Charm' among peonies in the traditional range of cool reds and pinks. 'Coral Charm' is a beautiful, relatively new color in peonies, but it does not go with 'Scarlet O'Hara' and 'Burma Ruby'! The rule of thumb is warm with warm, cool with cool. Pinks with blue in them are compatible with reds that have blue in them.

once you can see a difference between blues that lean toward violet, pure blues, and blues that lean toward green, you are doing well.

USING VALUE AND INTENSITY
IN THE GARDEN

Color is the first thing you notice about a flower. To a botanist, it is a clue to the identity of a species; to gardeners like me, it is one of the great attractions of gardening. But to painters of the Renaissance, color was less important than the skillful manipulation of values.

Leonardo da Vinci believed that creating the illusion of three-dimensional form by modeling with highlights and shadows was the measure of an artist. This technique, called *chiaroscuro*, took its name from the Italian words for *light* and *dark* and defined an era. Before rendering major works in color, many artists of that period made monochromatic studies to establish the most effective placement of lights and darks.

Controlling values is a way of establishing the foundation and framework of a composition. As the eye is drawn to the lightest areas first, highlights show you where to look and what is worth looking at. Darkness emphasizes important features by contrast.

Contrasts in value work the same way in the garden that they do in a painting. A dark background gives prominence to lighter forms in front of it; a light background creates interesting silhouettes. Evergreens such as yews, hollies, and hemlocks, with their dark green foliage and substantial size, come into their own in value contrasts and provide "bone structure" for a garden.

All gardens need a bit of structure and can make good use of evergreen walls. For example, there is nothing like a yew hedge to show off a perennial border. Against the firm contours and dark color of the hedge, you can appreciate the lighter skyline of the garden with its ups and downs and negative spaces. Conversely, a light background defines dark shapes. At Longwood Gardens in Kennett Square, Pennsylvania, a spring planting of pink and red tulips dramatizes dark, weighty cones of yew.

THIS PAGE: The evergreen yew hedge shows off the lighter skyline of the perennial border in Lynden Miller's Connecticut garden.

OPPOSITE: Pink and red tulips dramatize the dark, weighty cones of yew at Longwood Gardens in Kennett Square, Pennsylvania.

In the naturalistic garden illustrated here, the "walls" are informal plantings of rhododendrons, conifers, and deciduous shrubs. Against their darkness, *Hosta* with either white-edged leaves or light, bright, yellow-green foliage guide the steps of visitors along the garden path. At the far end, a pair of conifers stands out, like sentinels, against their lighter surroundings.

No one handled lights and darks in the garden better than Gertrude Jekyll. Being a former painter, she knew how to fill alcoves among rhododendrons with clouds of misty-white flowers and to place paler green ferns against masses of darker green foliage. Her use of contrasting values holds up even in the old black-and-white photos of her gardens in *Colour Schemes for the Flower Garden*.

THIS PAGE: Plants with lighter foliage lead the way along a path in Welsey Rouse's Connecticut garden.

OPPOSITE: The darker surrounding foliage shows off the pale green ferns at the Garden of Ideas in Ridgefield, Connecticut.

VALUE CONTRASTS HELP DEFINE SPACES

Designer and herbalist Ragna Goddard knows how to handle shadow and substance in a garden and shares her expertise through lectures and tours of her Sundial Gardens in Higganum, Connecticut. Here, the reassuring year-round presence of evergreens plays a crucial role in creating boundaries and defining spaces. Boxwood hedges establish a framework for the different gardens within them: the sundial garden, the topiary garden, and the knot garden. The plan is a grid pattern, linking the house to this series of green outdoor "rooms."

Evergreens delineate the walls and furnish the enclosed spaces with sculptural forms. In the case of the knot garden, evergreen herbs even carpet the floor. Set off by a light-gray fieldstone walk, meticulously sheared herbs—with contrasting light and dark foliage—trace the complex patterns derived from Persian rugs.

This garden is not dependent on colorful flowers for its beauty but on satisfying proportions, line, form, and contrasting values. At any time of year, highlights and shadows enliven the enclosed spaces and play across the cubes, globes, and topiary forms, emphasizing their restrained geometry.

Looking at Gardens in Black and White

Black-and-white photographs of colorful flower gardens are very educational. The hues in the middle of the light-to-dark scale, like red and red-orange, look the same as their green leaves. Yellow flowers, having a much lighter value than the reds and greens, stand out from their foliage. Blue and violet blossoms, on the other hand, virtually disappear.

At night, the value difference is even greater. Light colors shine forth, and darker shades vanish into Stygian blackness. White, of course, is the lightest color of all. Along with pastels, whites appear to advance toward the viewer; blues and violets recede.

Although yellow is the lightest, brightest hue—excluding white—it has the narrowest range of tints and shades. Reds have a wide range, from dark, rich shades of red to strong pinks to the

Seeing a garden in black and white reveals differences in color values.

White is the lightest of all values; blue and violet are darkest.

palest of pale blush-pinks. But yellow has a very limited range, basically, light yellow and dark yellow. Even dark yellow is considerably lighter than any of the dark shades of red, blue, green, and purple. Orange, like yellow, has fewer variations from light to dark than the other colors.

If you are ever tempted to try a flower bed in one color, you will quickly discover the importance of lights and darks. In the absence

of other hues, it takes a full range of tints, tones, and shades to keep the viewer's eye engaged. Like the monochromatic studies made by artists, flower beds limited to one color teach you to pay attention to values, along with sizes, shapes, and textures.

Modifying Intensity

Value is about degrees of light and dark, but intensity concerns "degrees of power." Hollandia Nursery, one of our Newtown, Connecticut garden centers, shows what pure, fully saturated colors at maximum power can do. In the display beds, massed annu-

TOP: Red glows in all its variety at Westpark in Munich, Germany. The range of yellow, however, is limited to light and dark.

als, in the strongest possible reds, the brightest yellows, the most vivid pinks, and the purest oranges, dare passersby to ignore them.

From May to October, a visit to Hollandia makes your heart sing. But in a small flower bed, so many intense colors at close range could be wearing. And that's where desaturated tints and tones come in—as arbitrators among powerful colors.

In painting, a dab of white added to intense, pure red results in a bright pink. But even bright pink does not make as strong a statement as bright red. It would, however, be at the high end of the intensity scale because there is still so much red in it. Blush-pink contains so little red that it falls much lower on the saturation scale.

Hollandia Nursery displays the power of fully saturated colors.

Dark red is a relatively pure color and, therefore, more intense than blush-pink. In between lie all those red tints, tones, and shades that are less altered than blush-pink but more altered than bright pink and dark red.

Any color can be grayed and reduced to a tone. Painters do it either by diluting the intense color, adding gray pigment, or mixing in a little of the complementary color. It is a curious fact that complementary colors, so vivid and mutually enhancing in juxtaposition, have the opposite effect when mixed together as pigment. Adding a little green to red tones down the red. Nature also seems to know this technique. Complementary green lies beneath the maroon leaves of canna 'Wyoming' and gives them their rich, deep tone of red.

The smoky blue of far-off mountains is also a tone, much altered and reduced in saturation by the bloom of distance, while the pure, intense blue of the night sky is a very dark shade. In the

The green in this canna leaf lowers the intensity of the red.

garden, it really doesn't matter which is a shade and which is a tone or what you call them. What does matter is that desaturated colors have a different quality from pure, fully saturated colors.

The natural world abounds in lovely, soft, indefinite tones. Traditional dyes produce similar hues called "sad colors." You could also describe them as neutrals: the colors of the winter landscape, of earth and stone, bark and branch. Low-intensity variations exist in every color. Desaturated tones of red and purple are found in the foliage of garden shrubs, such as smoke bush and Japanese barberry. And many of the gray-greens exhibited by our so-called silver-foliage plants are also tones.

In the garden, soft, grayed tones are useful either to subdue contrasts or to exploit them. Last year, I found a lone seedling of an

opium poppy that had pushed its way up through a clump of *Nepeta* 'Six Hill's Giant.' Surrounded by the mops of gray-green foliage and low intensity lavender-blue *Nepeta* flowers, one pure, bright pink flower leapt from obscurity to center stage. Never had a poppy looked so pink!

A reputedly true story, recounted in *J. M. W. Turner*, by Robert Kenner, reinforces the point. In the summer of 1832, Turner, the renowned British landscape painter, and his rival, John Constable, were exhibiting work at the Royal Academy. Constable's entry was a color-filled canvas of Waterloo Bridge; Turner's was a subdued seascape.

Fellow artist and contemporary C. R. Leslie described watching Turner, who studied the two paintings and then disappeared into the next room, reappearing with brush and palette. With a swift, sure hand, he laid a single dab of brilliant red paint, about the size of a quarter, on his gray sea. The impact of the intensity contrast made Constable's canvas pale into insignificance. "He has been here," said the disgruntled Constable, "and fired a gun."

NATURE AND ART
Looking at Color

THE ROMAN PHILOSOPHER SENECA claimed that "All art is but imitation of nature." Traditionally, artists have taken inspiration from the natural landscape, and gardeners, in turn, have been inspired by painters. For my part, the English poet and writer Walter Savage Landor said it all in the poem "I Strove with None": "Nature I loved; and next to Nature, Art."

For ideas on color, European painters of the nineteenth century are exciting and accessible. At that time, the art establishment favored politically correct subjects, a restrained use of color, and superior draftsmanship. J. M. W. Turner changed all that. While conventional artists depicted scenes from history and the Bible, Turner focused on light, color, and the out-of-doors.

Turner, *The Burning of the Houses of Lords and Commons, 1834,* 1835.

TURNER'S HOT HARMONIES

~

You don't have to know anything about art to respond to Turner's 1835 painting of England's Houses of Parliament being consumed by fire. The drama of the moment is spelled out in colors that pant with heat and urgency. Leaping orange and gold flames rise into the night sky, their reflections spreading across the Thames River from shore to shore.

In the painting, the hot color harmonies generate excitement. They do the same in a garden and in nature. Orange, red, and gold are the colors of sunsets and autumn leaves. In my fall garden, the Japanese shrub *Enkianthus campanulatus* bursts into flame in mid- to late October behind the yellow flowers of late-blooming witch hazel (*Hamamelis virginiana*). Daylilies in similar hues provide summer fireworks in my perennial border.

To create his fiery sunset color schemes, Turner combined new technology with the age-old technique of imitating nature. He experimented with the intense cadmium-based reds and yellows that had recently become available and made them more vibrant by surrounding them with cobalt blue and cobalt violet, also newly introduced colors.

At least one nineteenth-century British gardener saw the possibilities in these swirling harmonies of red, orange, and gold, framed by contrasting cool hues. Gertrude Jekyll was only eight years old when Turner died in 1851, but she had already begun drawing and painting, and she loved color. As a young woman and budding artist, she was immediately attracted to Turner's work and according to her biographer, Betty Massingham, spent "hours on end" copying his paintings.

Nor were the lessons she learned then forgotten. In middle age, when failing eyesight curtailed her own painting, the garden became her canvas. Turner's technique of embracing hot colors with cool, contrasting blues and purples found its way into her garden at Munstead Wood, Jekyll's home in Surrey, England.

The two ends of her main border were devoted to blues—pure blue at one end and violet-blue at the other, while the colors between became gradually stronger and hotter. Yellow proceeded from lemon to gold to orange to flame and, finally, crossed the bar into scarlet and crimson. From the conflagration in the middle, the hues reversed through warm to cool: orange to yellow to violet-blue.

I don't know what kind of a painter Jekyll was. But as a garden colorist, she must have been a genius to orchestrate all these hues into one sweeping symphony of color. The complexity of the scheme with its subtle gradations, leading from cool to warm to hot

Taking his cue from Nature, Turner juxtaposed warm reds and oranges with cool shades of violet. A gardener can do the same.

and back again, is far beyond most gardeners. But the lessons Jekyll learned from studying Turner should not be lost on the rest of us. To create excitement in a garden, try red and orange flowers with cool blues and violets for contrast. I know it works because this year, I used these colors in a container garden scheme on the terrace.

IMPRESSIONIST MOMENTS SPARKLE WITH LIGHT

~

Jekyll's mentor, Turner, is said to have fired the first shot in the nineteenth-century art revolution, but the French painters who followed

Monet, *Garden at Sainte-Adresse*, 1867.

him opened up with a full-scale barrage of new ideas about light and color. If you have an opportunity, visit the Metropolitan Museum of Art, in New York City and look for the impressionist paintings.

The impressionists illustrate everything a gardener needs to know about using color. Being in a room full of Monets or Renoirs is like being in a garden on a perfect summer afternoon. You can feel the warmth of the sun, and the colors are as fresh as the day they were applied to the canvas.

In 1867, Claude Monet captured just such a sparkling moment in *Garden at Sainte-Adresse*. At that time, he had not yet begun to dematerialize his subjects into shimmering studies of atmosphere. The colors are bright and lively, and the brush strokes, relatively conventional.

On a terrace overlooking the water, members of his family appear to be enjoying the sea air. In the foreground, shaded by a white parasol, Tante Lecadre relaxes in a garden chair. She is framed by a hot color harmony of brilliant red, orange, and yellow nasturtiums; red gladioli; and scarlet geraniums. These colors, all adjacent to each other on the color wheel, are linked together by their mutual warmth. While other members of the Monet family gaze peacefully out across the cool blue water, bright little flags overhead whip in the wind. Their pennants create lively diagonals that contrast with the level calm of the horizon.

On one side of the painting, the sea beyond the orange brick wall is an intense, deep blue. On the opposite side, red gladioli rise above the wall and stand out against a much greener blue sea—a subtle use of complementary contrasts. Although hot color harmonies predominate in the flower beds, there are plenty of complementary and near complementary contrasts between the flowers and their green leaves.

You could do far worse than to copy the colors and even some of the plants. For a bright, eye-catching summer garden, nothing is more welcoming and cheerful than red geraniums and red, orange, and yellow nasturtiums.

Although Monet's contrasts are bold and the colors intense, it is Tante Lecadre's white parasol that commands our attention. The first time I saw the painting, the prominence of the parasol confirmed my growing suspicion that white, in the garden, is not a conciliatory color among other hues. Instead, it serves as a very effective attention-getting device.

The white parasol in the painting behaves exactly the way a dense clump of pure white *Boltonia asteroides* behaves in my perennial border. White demands the viewer's attention by virtue of extreme contrast. And in a colorful border, that solid patch of white creates an unwelcome distraction. But in the painting, the parasol performs a valuable service. It leads the eye on a vigorous diagonal path that injects vitality and energy into the otherwise placid scene.

THIS PAGE: Red geraniums and red-orange, and yellow nasturtiums echo Monet's *Garden at Sainte-Adresse.*

OPPOSITE, TOP: Just like Tante Lecadre's parasol, white gets the attention.

BOTTOM: Monet's *The Artist's Garden at Giverney* from 1900 inspires many gardeners with its harmonies of blue, pink, green, violet, and purple.

Monet, being a passionate gardener himself, devoted a great deal of canvas to gardens. From the time he settled in Giverny until his death in 1926, the now famous garden was his only model. Fortunately, it continues to flourish, luring thousands of visitors every year.

Although he loved bright, daring colors, many of Monet's garden paintings are done in silvery harmonies of blue, pink, green, violet, and purple. Indeed, these are the colors most often associated with his work. And they are the hues that most often appeal to gardeners.

VAN GOGH: A STUDY
IN CONTRASTS

If Monet's Giverny paintings show gardeners how to create exquisitely modulated harmonies, the work of troubled, Dutch-born Vincent van Gogh provides a mother lode of contrasts. During the years he spent in the south of France, he produced green fields spattered with dazzling red poppies, blue skies blazing down on restless acres of golden grain, fields of quivering buttercups set off by ditches full of purple irises.

Van Gogh worked with all the classic complementary pairs and near complements, knowing that they strengthen each other by contrast: red and green, blue and orange, yellow and purple, yellow and blue. He returned to this last combination again and again. Even in self-portraits of this period, the major hues are usually blue, yellow, and orange.

RIGHT: Van Gogh, *Self Portrait with a*

Straw Hat, 1888.

Gardeners are drawn to these colors, too. Indeed, any color scheme that makes a painting interesting, exciting, or beautiful can be translated to the garden or terrace container.

DISCOVERING NATURE'S COLOR SCHEMES

When I returned to painting after a hiatus of several years, I discovered, among other things, that I painted like a gardener, not an artist. My love affair was, and is, with the natural world and with what I see. When I paint flowers, gardens, landscapes, even portraits, I am not trying to express anything except passionate admiration for the work of nature. The subject is the purpose of the painting.

I borrowed the blues and oranges of fall for my summer border.

Artists have a different agenda. The subject is less important than the expressive power of paint. Although the contrasts that emerged in van Gogh's late work came straight from the countryside outside Arles, he didn't *copy* what he saw. Instead, he *translated* the colors into highly emotional landscapes, portraits, and self-portraits. He spent hours mulling over the complementary relationship between the golden fields of the Midi and the bright blue sky overhead. In W. H. Auden's *Van Gogh: A Self-Portrait* (a collection of his letters) Van Gogh

wrote: "*There is no blue without yellow and without orange*, and if you put in blue, then you must put in yellow, and orange too, mustn't you?"

I don't think like that. When I see these colors in the October landscape, all I can think of is how heavenly they look together. And when it comes to transferring them to the garden, I simply copy what I have seen and enjoyed. You don't have to go to the south of France to see yellow, orange, and blue in the landscape. If you live in the northeast, you don't have to do anything, except wait until fall. Gardeners used to avoid these glorious colors. But recently, orange, yellow, and gold have been rehabilitated, and hot is "in." In my long border, you will find autumn's color scheme in full swing in July. And to partner the orange daylilies, you see the complementary blue of globe thistles (*Echinops ritro* 'Taplow's Blue').

Learning to See Color Around You

Borrowing color schemes from the landscape and using them in flower beds is far easier than painting, and I finally abandoned the brush for the trowel. But I have never regretted a moment spent painting. It sharpened my eyes to the world around me and to nature's color schemes.

The complementary contrast of purple and yellow is one of nature's finest contributions to the summer landscape. In August, sunny Connecticut fields boast great sweeps of goldenrod interrupted by tall clumps of purple New York ironweed (*Vernonia noveboracensis*). This stalwart native soars above the seas of gold on strong stems topped with flat clusters of fuzzy, deep-purple flowers. The goldenrods are a variable lot, with species that extend the

Purple and yellow stand out in the summer landscape.

A GARDENER'S INTERPRETATION OF A MEADOW

Connecticut gardener Mary Stambaugh has taken a typical field as her model for a wonderful meadow garden. Here, you will find the purple and gold scheme in bloom for weeks on end. Her meadow covers more than two acres. A broad, closely mowed path through the middle is thronged on either side with native grasses and wildflowers. Sunflowers and *Rudbeckia* intermingle with stands of goldenrod, interrupted here and there by vigorous clumps of ironweed and Joe Pyeweed. The wildness is gently restrained from leaning too far into the path by a rustic fence made of branches from an old cherry tree.

Mary calls her creation "a gardener's interpretation of a meadow" because she includes suitable nonnatives, such as dainty purple meadow rue (*Thalictrum rochebrunianum*) from Japan and orange tiger lilies that fit in with the purple and gold theme and have the feeling of authenticity.

season from midsummer into October. New England asters replace
ironweed as the purple partner for the later-blooming goldenrods.

Colors in Flowers

Beginning in September, nature offers up dozens of examples of
another complementary contrast, red and green, provided by berries
ripening among green leaves. On female plants of sumac (*Rhus
glabra*), large, upright clusters of suede-textured fruits mature to
dark red; and the smooth, shiny fruits of winterberry (*Ilex verticil-
lata*) turn bright scarlet.

In the garden, the Christmas card scheme of red and green is one
of the best. Don't be put off by its familiarity. Nature isn't, and

Monet wasn't. Nor are some of today's most creative gardeners. Wesley Rouse, landscape designer and owner of Pine Meadow Gardens, Inc., welcomes visitors to his home with cascades of crimson begonias, glowing against their dark green foliage. Occasionally his beautiful private garden in Southbury, Connecticut is open for tours.

Not all of nature's color combinations are as vivid and visible as red berries against green leaves. Some are hidden inside flowers. To find them, you have to look at every part of the blossom: the veins and backs of the petals, the curious architecture of the reproductive parts, even the pollen. A surprise awaits you inside the narrow, yellow-green bells of *Nicotiana langsdorffii*, where you will find anthers bearing sky-blue pollen. On a large, obvious scale, sky blue and yellow-green are the colors of spring. The deciduous trees sport chartreuse tassels and tiny new leaves that stand out against the blue sky.

These colors are wonderful together in the garden. One gardener saw possibilities in the combination and encouraged the chartreuse bracts of *Euphorbia seguieriana* to grow up through a blue lacecap hydrangea (*Hydrangea macrophylla*).

The tulip tree (*Liriodendron tulipifera*) plays hard to get. Its flowers open on the upper branches, but perfect blossoms do fall to the ground, and they are exquisite. Pick one up and examine the cup-shaped flower. It consists of six creamy-green petals marked with orange, encircling a narrow green cone, which in turn, is sur-

Nature's spring color scheme of yellow-green with sky-blue can be interpreted with plants.

rounded by yellow anthers. The same colors make a lovely garden composition: orange *Kniphofia* accenting a group of false sunflowers against a green background.

Most flowers are neither as secretive as the *Nicotiana* nor as inaccessible as those of the tulip tree. In fact, some flaunt their color schemes. The coneflower (*Echinacea purpurea*) holds up its handsome daisylike blossoms for all to admire the prominent orange cones among mauve-pink rays.

Nature's orange and mauve combination can also be mimicked in the garden.

The success of the coneflower's offbeat color combination illustrates a pet theory of mine: color schemes that work in a blossom will probably work in the garden, no matter how unusual or surprising.

The coneflower scheme of pink and orange is not for the fainthearted, but that's the last thing you could call Connecticut gardener Kathy Loomis. She loves color and is not timid about using it. In her garden, a mass of bright orange butterfly weed (*Asclepias tuberosa*) stands proudly, shoulder to shoulder, with its mauve-pink cousin, swamp milkweed *Asclepias incarnata*.

The flowers of European mullein (*Verbascum chaixii*) boast another interesting combination: bright yellow and dusky pink. The same colors enrich a perennial border at Rouse's Pine Meadow Gardens, where smoky heads of Joe Pyeweed set off loose, dainty clusters of *Patrinia triloba*.

Bright yellow and dusky pink are an interesting combination, but for something more daring try crimson and pink together.

If the combination of yellow and dusky pink is too tame for you, how about crimson and pink together? Nature does it in the fanciful blossoms of the red orchid cactus (*Nopalxochia ackermannii*), a popular houseplant. Many long petals, like strips of crimson satin, surround the pink pistil and a dependent cluster of pink anthers. In this garden version of the same color scheme, narrow pink spikes of *Celosia spicata* turn up in the unlikely company of a huge red dahlia. If nature dares to use red and pink together, why shouldn't gardeners?

HARMONY AND CONTRAST

How Color Schemes Work

IF YOU ARE WONDERING WHY HARMONY and contrast turn up again and again in paintings, there is a reason. They work. And they work because the relationships between colors make sense. It is only logical that colors sharing a common pigment will be more compatible than those with nothing in common. Thus, harmonies are created from colors that are more alike than different and contrasts are created using colors that have dissimilarities.

All color schemes are, of course, based on the natural arrangement of hues in the rainbow. The color wheel follows this natural order but makes the relationships between colors easier to understand by isolating individual hues. Their positions on the color wheel show you which are alike and which are different. Success with color boils down to recognizing likenesses and differences, and it is easier to show them than to explain them. But here goes.

HARMONIES

~

Harmonies are family affairs based on likeness. Although the extended red family includes all the colors that have red in them, red with either red-violet or red-orange constitutes the closest family unit. Expanding the unit to include all three reds—red, red-violet, and red-orange—puts a slight strain on family ties because of the difference between red-violet and red-orange. The easiest harmonies to put together are pairs of adjacent colors. There is always a sense of rightness about them.

All color families lend themselves to harmonies of two or possibly three adjacent hues. For longer sequences, the reds, violets, blues, and greens offer the widest range of tints, tones, and shades. However, longer sequences of closely related hues are the hardest to pull off. You have to recognize very slight differences between the colors, and that takes an educated eye.

As the pleasure of harmony lies in a seamless progression of similar but different hues, the challenge is to lessen differences grad-

ually. As mentioned previously, Gertrude Jekyll was a master of
close harmonies and introduced changes in color "by degrees." In
Colour Schemes for the Flower Garden, she describes sorting geraniums very carefully by color and arranging them in a harmonious
sequence from salmon-pink to pure scarlet: "I have great pleasure
in putting together Omphale, palest salmon-pink; Mrs. Lawrence,
a shade deeper; Mrs. Cannell, a salmon-scarlet approaching the
quality of colour of Phlox Coquelicot; and leading these by degrees
to the pure, good scarlet of Paul Crampel."

MAXIMUM CONTRAST: COMPLEMENTARY COLORS

~

The essence of harmony is likeness, but the soul of contrast is difference. The greater the difference, the greater the contrast. Complementary pairs, like red and green, yellow and violet, blue and orange, are compelling because they are complete opposites. Yet, optically, you can't have one without the other.

If you stare fixedly at the color red, then look at a blank white surface, you will see a glowing ghost of green, its complement. This phenomenon takes about twenty seconds to work. Try it with the red berries of the *Viburnum* against the green background of its own leaves. After a period of intense staring, look at a piece of white

paper, and you will see pale, phosphorescent greenish berries against a pink background.

This optical illusion is called the *afterimage*, and it works with all colors. Stare at a sheet of yellow paper, then look at a white surface, and a luminous violet afterimage will appear. Violet is the complement of yellow. Try the same thing with blue, which has a complementary golden-orange afterimage.

Although science does not yet have all the answers, it is believed that this curious apparition is like a screen saver for the eye. The theory is that staring at any given color is tiring. Seeking relief, the eye demands the opposite experience. If it is overexposed to red, it wants green; if it is tired of yellow, it needs violet; if it wearies of blue, it demands orange; and if it has had enough of white, it wants black.

Although red and green, yellow and violet, and blue and orange do *compliment* each other, the meaning of *complement* has to do with completion, not flattery. *Webster's New World Dictionary* defines a complement as "that which completes." So Vincent van Gogh was right. If you use blue in a painting, orange is present, even if it is not visible. Blue and orange complete each other and are, therefore, inseparable. Side by side, they are doubly powerful. Having encountered blue, your eye already *wants* orange, and vice versa.

If successful color harmonies are like families, complementary pairs and other color schemes built on differences are like strangers at a party. Contrasting personalities provide an element of excitement. But you don't want bedlam. There is nothing worse at a party than too many demanding guests, all competing for attention. The same is true in a garden: you don't want too many extreme contrasts battling it out in a perennial border.

This is where the color wheel can be of real practical help. It shows you how all colors are related to one another. From their relationships, you know which are likely to get along well, being members of the same family, and which are opposites.

BASIC COLOR SCHEMES

The color wheel also shows you how to venture beyond the tried and true complementary pairs and sister acts of two adjacent colors. It diagrams eight specific color schemes, all worth an experiment in the garden. The silver garden at Longwood Gardens in Kennett Square, Pennsylvania illustrates an achromatic scheme. *Achromatic* means "without color," and technically speaking, black, white, and gray are colorless, although grays in nature are always tinted with other hues.

Silver garden, Longwood Gardens, Pennsylvania.

A *monochromatic* scheme sticks to one color but includes all its variations. Red gardens are popular and a good choice because red boasts such a wide range of tints, tones, and shades. A red corner of Helen Bodian's garden, in Duchess County, New York, shows you how winning a monochromatic scheme can be. The reds run the gamut from a tint of pink to pure vivid primary red to dark, velvety shades of red to resonant tones of maroon. And there is plenty of variety in flower size, shape, and plant habit. You will be seeing more of this garden later.

The *analogous* scheme is based on a sequence of three or four adjacent and, therefore, closely related hues. And they must fit into a ninety-degree angle on the color wheel. Crimson—the cool red— along with red-violet and violet fit within a ninety-degree angle.

These are the colors used in Richard Copeland's Connecticut garden, which you will soon visit.

The extended red family of crimson, red-violet, and violet also includes cool tints of pink, mauve, and lavender, all the colors of this beautiful rose display at the Munich Botanic Garden, in Germany.

The rest of the color schemes on the color wheel are based on varying degrees of contrast. Dynamic complementary pairs are already familiar. But a *"split complement"* involves three colors: a key color, plus the colors on either side of its complement. Here's a color scheme with just as much pizzazz as any complementary pair.

In this garden version of a split complementary scheme, the key color is red-violet; its complement is yellow-green; and the colors on either side are yellow and green. When Geranium 'Ann Folkard,' with stinging magenta flowers, ventures boldly among the yellow spikes of Kniphofia against a background of green and yellow-green foliage, the effect is electrifying.

The remaining schemes on the color wheel are almost self-explanatory. *Diads*, *triads*, and *tetrads* are just what they sound like, schemes involving two, three, and four hues. *Diads* are two colors separated from each other by one color, illustrated here by red-violet *Geranium* 'Ann Folkard' with blue-violet salvia. Red-violet and blue-violet form a family unit but are different enough from each other to provide an element of contrast.

Triads, made up of three colors equally spaced from each other, can be either contrasting or harmonious. The greater the distance between the colors, the greater the contrast. Red, yellow, and blue, the three primaries, with no pigment in common and three colors separating them, result in a highly contrast-

ing triad. Red, orange, and yellow, on the other hand, have pigment in common and are only one color apart, which makes them more harmonious.

Red, yellow, and blue make up the most striking triad; shown here at the Institute for Ecosystem Studies in Millbrook, New York.

In the garden, color schemes combining three or four adjacent hues with the complement of one of them have it all: the adjacent hues produce harmony, and the complement of any one of them produces a degree of contrast but not too much.

If a color combination needs a name, you could call this one an *analogous-complementary* scheme. In a Massachusetts conifer garden, the appearance of the first red-orange maple leaves creates a complementary contrast with the blue-green spruces. At the same time, the presence of green in all the conifer colors unites them in an analogous harmony. This is the best of both worlds.

Actually, all gardens, even monochromatic gardens, contain both harmony and con-

The best of both worlds in Nancy Britz's Massachusetts garden. Her scheme combines both contrast and harmony.

trast. Willy-nilly, Nature provides green leaves to cool the hottest red garden; and flowers with yellow centers bring a touch of warmth to the coolest blue garden. With Nature playing her part, most color schemes work to some extent.

GARDEN COLOR SCHEMES

Thematic Gardens

To many gardeners, harmony means flower colors in a range of cool pinks and blue-violets combined with silver foliage. But hot reds and oranges combined with foliage colors that have a warm undercurrent are just as harmonious. Harmony is a matter of keeping colors within the family.

Contrast results in color schemes of a very different character. Contrasting colors are used for emphasis and to attract attention. Often, they astonish and delight viewers by their audacity.

Whichever you prefer, contrast or harmony, the important thing is to find a purposeful, personally satisfying way of combining flower and foliage colors.

COOL COLOR HARMONIES

~

I have admired Lynden Miller's Connecticut garden for years. It is a garden that fits any definition of harmony. Always beautiful, always confined to a limited range of hues between blue and crimson, it still surprises me with new plants and deft accommodations to time.

The colors and their proportions are perfect. Clear pinks and deep tones of red and purple are repeated throughout, along with

Cool colors predominate in this lovely border.

accents of violet, blue-violet, and blue. The dominant hues, with all their attendant tints and shades, provide the underlying theme of likeness—the *sine qua non* of harmony.

In addition to pink phlox, the indispensable perennials for midsummer are *Echinacea purpurea* and, in the foreground, blue oat grass (*Helictotrichon sempervirens*). In the background, airy lavender meadow rue (*Thalictrum rochebrunianum*) and tall *Miscanthus sinensis* 'Gracillimus' and *Miscanthus sinensis* 'Variegatus' stand out against the meticulously sheared yew hedge. Solid globes of red barberry (*Berberis thunbergii* 'Rose Glow') and the leafy, upright stems of purple smokebush (*Cotinus coggygria* 'Royal Purple') forge connecting links of red and purple.

Miller came to garden design by way of art. Trained as a painter, she had been working professionally for eighteen years when she

became involved in the restoration project that launched her design career—the Conservatory Garden in New York City's Central Park.

Today, she is an award-winning designer of public gardens. When aspiring garden designers ask her for advice, she encourages them to look at paintings and to study art history. "You should go to museums," says Lynden, "and see how people put paintings together because it's just the same as in the garden—line, form, texture, and proportion of colors."

Another beautiful Connecticut garden has its roots in a deep love and appreciation of art. Richard Copeland and his French wife,

Martine, are connoisseurs and collectors. And their garden reflects their interest and knowledge.

On a level terrace built into their steep hillside, Richard has laid out a series of ornamental flower beds. The beds are edged with boxwood and arranged on either side of the long axis, which makes the garden appear deceptively spacious. The design was inspired by the parterres of France and is intended to remind Martine of home. Matching beds furnished with trios of slender arborvitae, *Thuja occidentalis* 'Degroots Spire,' reinforce the French connection. Although arborvitae is a familiar native tree, its narrow, upright growth habit suggests that of cypress from the south of France.

For flower colors, Richard turned to the work of Claude Monet. With eyes educated by years of looking at artwork, he proceeded to assemble a closely coordinated sequence of hues worked out with roses and annuals. Harmonizing shades and tints of crimson, pink, and violet fill a long bed on top of the retaining wall. In the small parterres, red, pink, and blue annuals surround standard roses. All the colors lie on the cool side of the color wheel between crimson and blue.

HOT COLOR HARMONIES

Elisabeth Sheldon's hot garden in upstate New York is startlingly different from the Copeland's garden and from Miller's border. But the colors are just as closely related and harmonious. Only this time, a different wedge of the color wheel has been explored.

To segregate the fiery colors from her main border, which is devoted to cool pastels, she built them a little enclosure of their own surrounded by a cedar fence. The warm tones of the weathered cedar fit in with the pinkish hue of the paving blocks she used for the paths and small patio. Flaming cannas and dahlias, golden rudbeckias, and marigolds are the heart and soul of the hot garden.

I was not surprised to learn from Sheldon's book, *A Proper Garden*, that she had studied painting at the Art Institute of Chicago and the University of Chicago. It shows in her repetition of color and form and the progressions of closely allied hues.

Elisabeth Sheldon's "hot" New York garden.

Photographers, like artists and art collectors, are in the business of looking, which is one reason that Helen Bodian's red, orange, and purple garden succeeds. She is a professional photographer and a serious amateur gardener. Tired of pale, tame hues, Bodian decided to celebrate the new millennium with hot colors.

Her hot spot lies along the north side of the greenhouse and is enclosed by a stucco wall. Inside, orange velvet *Tithonia rotundifolia* and dark-leaved cannas with red and orange flowers stand tall above the scarlet dahlias. Touches of chartreuse appear among the outrageous crimson *amaranths* (*Amaranthus caudatus*), red castor beans, and the burgundy-and-purple foliage of coleus.

Even though the color scheme is based, for the most part, on hot hues, it produces a very different impression from the bright fireworks of the Sheldon garden. A greater number of colors are involved in Bodian's scheme: orange and red-orange; deep shades of scarlet and crimson; plum, purple, and even a touch of deep blue.

The lavish use of dark foliage and gradual shifts in color temperature succeed in harmonizing this sequence of strong hues. The desaturated foliage tones are particularly useful. Colors that are very different from one another at full strength become more compati-

Touches of chartreuse brighten the deep foliage tones in Helen Bodian's gardens.

ble with every degree of desaturation. In Bodian's intriguingly complex scheme, the deep-red foliage tones provide a thread of likeness that weaves all the colors together.

If you look again at the photos of Miller's garden, you will notice that yellow is missing. Actually, a single clump of yellow daylilies does light up the darkness under the crabapple tree. But the yellow is a cool, lemon yellow, not a brassy orange-yellow.

Sheldon also admitted lemon-yellow and even touches of crimson into her cool mixed border. But the warm scarlets and golden yellows were dispatched to her home for hot colors, where they both lean contentedly toward orange. In the Copeland garden, yellow, orange, and scarlet are absent altogether, leaving only the cool crimson reds, cool pinks, and hues with blue in them.

Likeness is the underlying principle in these gardens. Harmonies are like the card game Happy Families. Keep the suits together—like with like: warm with warm; cool with cool.

COMPLEMENTARY CONTRASTS

In the garden, contrasts are easier to handle than harmonies. While, harmonies emphasize likeness, contrasts celebrate difference. Lying directly opposite each other on the color wheel, complementary colors earn a ten on the contrast scale. They represent maximum contrast and are the cheerful, decorative, greeting card colors that you see in action every day. But complementary colors can also express a darker side of life.

Van Gogh, *Night Café*, 1888.

In one of his late paintings, Vincent van Gogh pitted complements and other dissimilar colors against each other to express his inner turmoil. To pay his rent, he did a painting of his landlord's cafe, which he described as the "ugliest" piece of work he had ever done. "Everywhere," he wrote, "there is a clash and contrast of the most disparate reds and greens."

Extreme contrasts cause turmoil in the garden, too. Although contrast is a wonderful technique for creating colorful containers and enlivening beds and borders, too much of a good thing can result in a visually exhausting garden. Nothing is more effective, however, than complementary pairs modified by tints, tones, and shades of both colors.

Expanded Complementary Pairs

For fun one summer, I devoted my containers to paired complements and their relations. In large, matching pots, I explored a range of reds and greens, expanded and enriched with tones and shades of maroon, bronze, and contrasting tints of green. 'Red King Humbert' cannas ruled by virtue of their impressive stature, scarlet flowers, and large, dark-red leaves. At their feet, coleus, with mahogany foliage edged in acid green, prostrated itself in a suitable manner, and bronze fennel played court jester. The tall wispy fennel, with its fragile clusters of chartreuse flowers, bowed and scraped among the canna stalks.

The tints, shades, and tones of red and green balanced the difference in hues by providing harmonious similarities and contrasting accents. The coleus leaves picked up but deepened the red tone of the canna foliage, and both set off the light yellow-green rims of the coleus. Yellow-green appeared again in the fennel's dainty flower clusters, and the threadlike bronze foliage echoed the color of the canna leaves.

My pots that year were a great success. In fact, Peter Wooster bestowed upon them the highest accolade. Gazing up at the towering 'Red King Humbert' cannas, he narrowed his eyes and said, "Those pots should be arrested!"

Cannas and coleus provide tints, tones, and shades of complementary red and green.

A TAPESTRY OF CONTRASTS AND HARMONIES

Although my friend Peter Wooster claims to be a color anarchist, his garden is a rich tapestry of contrasts and harmonies woven together with mellow foliage tones of green, yellow-green, bronze, purple, and maroon. If he is to be believed, his color schemes are largely unplanned. But I know that their spontaneity is subject to careful editing. I also know that he has an infallible eye and is a ruthless editor.

The now familiar red-and-green contrast appears often in Wooster's garden, in part because of his passion for amaranths. Last summer, a tall amaranth with upright crimson flowers met its reflection in the tight crimson buds of an old-fashioned shrub rose. Red also reverberated in the amaranth foliage, and the surrounding greenery provided the perfect complementary setting.

Although not as dramatic, the yellow-and-violet scheme, combined with tints of yellow and yellow-green, proved as versatile and effective as the red-and-green combination. I worked out two yellow-and-violet arrangements, using different plants and different container styles.

For a spiky shape to lend distinction and provide height in a shallow bowl, nine inches (22.5 cm) deep and twenty-four inches (60 cm) across, I recruited yucca 'Bright Edge' from the garden. Its green blades with yellow margins rose from among the deep-purple

leaves and trailing stems of *Tradescantia pallida* 'Purple Heart.' Pale yellow-green *Helichrysum* 'Limelight' and a variegated *Lantana* with yellow flowers mingled with the *Tradescantia*'s leafy stems and tumbled over the sides of the bowl.

These colors are very similar to another combination I saw in Wooster's garden. *Nicotiana langsdorffii* showered its little yellow-green bells in front of tall stems of *Verbena bonariensis* bearing mauve flowers. The bright yellow in his complementary scheme was supplied by variegated *Abutilon*. And the bright tints and hues were set off by dark red-purple *Perilla frutescens*.

In the same vein, I chose a canna with yellow-and-green variegated leaves for the centerpiece of my biggest pot and, again, used *Helichrysum* 'Limelight' to drape over the edge. To make the composition look more like a garden scene, I arranged smaller containers of single, bright-yellow 'Disco' marigolds around the base of the canna, along with pots of *Bidens ferulifolia* 'Golden Goddess.' Heliotrope served as an intermediate step between the tall canna and the low-growing plants and provided the necessary purple foil for the yellows and yellow-greens.

Degrees of Contrast

Putting together contrasting hues is pretty straightforward. But there can be different degrees of contrast. On a scale from one to ten,

the degree of contrast between red and orange is about one. They are more alike than different because they are only one color apart on the color wheel, and orange is half red. Red and yellow, on the other hand, have no pigment in common, are three colors apart, and are about an eight in terms of contrast. Although both are warm colors, their differences outweigh their likeness.

Contrasts of Value and Intensity

Besides contrasts determined by the position of hues on the color wheel, there are also contrasts of value and of intensity. In the summer when I look out of my office window, the most striking contrast is one of value. The light yellow-green foliage of a golden black locust (*Robinia pseudoacacia* 'Frisia') stands out vividly against the dark wall of forest trees.

A golden false cypress (*Chamaecyparis pisifera* 'Filifera Aurea') fifty feet (15 meters) away repeats the yellow-green theme but in a lower key. Even though the conifer is much larger, it shows up less because the color of its foliage is only a dim echo of the locust's bright, fully saturated gold. In the winter, however, when the locust is bare and leafless, the conifer comes into its own, and their roles are reversed.

The false cypress stands out against the gray forest trees, and the naked locust disappears into the background. In his 1957 classic, *This Hill, This Valley*, nature writer Hal Borland made a telling observation about the winter landscape: "Color becomes relative as

The yellow-green foliage contrasts with the dark green of the forest trees.

In summer, the bright foliage of the golden black locust on the right outshines the golden conifer on the left.

the seasons shift. Brilliance is less a matter of color itself than one of contrast." A contrast of intensity.

In the foreground of my office view, a single clump of *Yucca filamentosa* 'Golden Sword' almost succeeds in stealing the locust's summer thunder. Planted in an island bed in front of a low mound of *Chamaecyparis pisifera* 'Aurea Nana,' the shining rapiers of the yucca stand out because they are so much lighter and brighter than the evergreen foliage behind them.

In the winter, the conifer comes into its own while the deciduous locust vanishes into the background.

Now several years old, 'Golden Sword' thrusts its yellow blades, narrowly edged in green, upward and outward. You can't miss them because they are so different in form, as well as color, from the soft, dull mass of old gold *Chamaecyparis* foliage. This pair illustrates three different kinds of contrast: of plant habit, value, and intensity.

6

FROM COLLAGE TO CONTAINERS

Experimenting with Color

THE WONDERFUL THING ABOUT GARDENING is that even a complete beginner can dig a hole, stick in a plant, and get a thrill out of it. But to use color in the garden skillfully enough to find it thrilling takes time.

Until I discovered the joys of container gardening in the mid-eighties, my color experiments were put to the test on site and in the ground. Trying out different combinations in containers saved a great deal of time and trouble. But experimenting with paper collage proved an even more energy-efficient first step.

PAPER AND PLANTS

I now teach a color workshop based upon paper collage. Some examples are shown here. All you need is a selection of old gardening catalogs, some paint chips, colored paper in a rainbow of rich hues, glue sticks, and scissors. You will find that paper collage offers you a new way to look at color. Most gardeners are primarily concerned with plants; color is an afterthought. Assembling a collage forces you to think of the colors first and plants second.

If you are at a loss for somewhere to start, try copying Jeni Webber's floral color wheel, on page 5. Jeni used real flowers and leaves; you will be using photos of flowers and foliage. Remember her advice about starting with a wide range of colors from which to choose.

Beginning at the top of the circle, pick out a cool red and a warm red—cool to the left; warm to the right. Next, going clockwise from the warm red, look for a red that has more orange in it; then, one that is beginning to look more orange than red; and finally, a pure orange. On the other side of orange, you want an orange that has a bit of yellow in it, and so forth.

Try to make the transitions as gradual as possible. This is what color harmonies are about—progressions of closely related hues. You will find yourself constantly making comparisons and debating which yellow to put where. Does this one lean a little toward orange or has it a cool green tinge to it? Comparing colors teaches you to look more closely. With practice, you begin to *see* that this yellow is warmer than that.

Don't get bogged down in trying to be artistic. The purpose of this exercise is to learn by and from looking; the purpose of the next is to help you find your own color "voice."

A color notebook is a natural for gardeners. Only instead of plant habits, bloom dates, and wish lists, it contains photos from catalogs and gardening magazines, postcards from art exhibits, swatches of fabric, and scraps of colored paper. It is a way of raising your color consciousness and discovering what you really like.

THE CONTAINER GARDEN

~

Container gardening is the next step. It allows you to grow plants, get your hands dirty, and experiment with colors—still without digging beds and investing in hardy perennials. The only downside is that it can be addictive. I started with a few pots of geraniums and graduated to an army of containers filled every summer with new and different plants. In a collection of containers, you can grow more kinds of plants in a single season than a perennial gardener can grow in the ground in years. The secret is to use annuals and tender perennials.

Container gardening releases you from the limitations of your local hardiness zone. Zone numbers are based on annual minimum temperatures—the lower the number, the colder the temperatures. My garden is in Zone 6, with yearly minimum temperatures ranging from approximately 0 degrees Fahrenheit to −10 degrees Fahrenheit.

The description "tender perennial" is used here to indicate plants native to Zones 9 and 10, where winter temperatures rarely fall below freezing. Any plant that germinates, matures, flowers lavishly, then dies—all in one season—is considered an annual. Many plants that originate as perennials in frost-free zones can be grown as annuals in the northern zones. A few plants, like petunias, nicotianas, and snapdragons can survive mild winters in the northern zones.

Gardening with annuals and tender perennials lends itself to experimentation because you are never stuck with the consequences. Annuals obligingly succumb to the first frost. Tender perennials can be wintered over as houseplants or left to the same fate. Because container schemes are temporary, anything goes. You can afford to take risks and be reckless in your choice of colors and plants. You have nothing to lose but your inhibitions.

Full-scale gardening in containers.

When it comes to putting your color schemes together, there are two basic approaches. You can put together a number of plants in one container or you can pot individual plants and arrange them in a group. The advantage of individually potted plants is that you can shift the colors around until you are satisfied with your scheme.

Either way, containers limit the opportunities to go astray. You can only fit so many plants in a pot. Fewer plants and fewer colors mean fewer mistakes. But there are also fewer distractions to take your mind off an unfortunate combination of colors.

In a garden, colors rarely clash because they are buffered by distance and masses of green leaves. In a container, the hues are cheek by jowl and viewed at close range. When they clash, you know it.

COLOR COMPATIBILITY

One summer, I fell in love with Persian shield (*Strobilanthes dyerianus*), a striking foliage plant from Southeast Asia with iridescent purple-pink leaves. Having succumbed to its cool, shimmering beauty, I found I had nowhere to put it and wound up adding it to an existing plant combination.

The Persian shield's companions were a fringed bleeding heart, *Dicentra* 'Luxuriant,' borrowed for the summer from the shade garden. Its cool-pink flowers went beautifully with the purple of *Tradescantia pallida* 'Purple Heart' and with the pink in the foliage of a variegated sweet potato vine (*Ipomoea batatas* 'Pink Frost'). By a stroke of luck, the Persian shield might have been made for this scheme.

But instead of leaving well enough alone, I stuck a new coleus in with them. It had very dark red leaves, which might have worked had the red been a cool hue. But the bronze-red was a disaster and had to be removed. That's how I discovered that warm and cool red tones don't go together any better than warm and cool pink tints.

I learned also that dark foliage is sometimes deceptive. The leaf surface may be one color and the underside another, in which case,

The cool, shimmering beauty of Persian shield.

Cool versus warm in containers.

the most accurate test of color temperature is the underside. Determining which of the dark tones are warm and which are cool is the key to using them effectively.

Compare the two photographs above. One features the dark red-purple foliage of *Tradescantia* 'Purple Heart'; the other, the dark-red foliage of *Hibiscus acetosella* 'Red Shield.' One is a cool tone; the other, a warm tone.

The leaves of the hibiscus are red on top and a warm tone of earthy orange underneath. Their warmth makes them good company for scarlet geraniums and foliage plants combining red and yellow-green.

The purple-and-pink scheme is cool throughout. The underside of the *Tradescantia* foliage has a distinct blue cast. And even the

BEGINNING A CONTAINER GARDEN

To start an experimental container garden, you need a variety of pots, tubs, and window boxes. My biggest pots, which are twenty inches (50 cm) high and from eighteen inches (45 cm) to twenty-four inches (60 cm) across, are reserved for cannas and other statuesque plants. You have to match the ultimate size of the plant to the pot. For soil, you can use any standard potting mix, as long as it drains quickly.

The only exacting maintenance chore is providing water, every day if necessary. Watering is weather dependent. The hotter the temperature, the more often you have to water. The size and material of the container also affect watering. Small containers dry out faster than large ones; water evaporates more quickly from porous containers than from nonporous containers; and hanging baskets dry out in a heartbeat because every surface is exposed to the sun and wind.

green foliage of *Dicentra* 'Luxuriant' leans toward blue rather than toward yellow. Now, try to imagine switching the hibiscus and the *Tradescantia*. Such an exchange would spoil both schemes.

You can get away with incompatibilities in a garden and at a distance, but not up close in a container. That's why container color schemes are such good eye training. And they are such fun because there is never any harm done. Errors of judgment are easily remedied. If there are several plants in a pot, take out the offenders and put them somewhere else. If your scheme is a grouping of pots, just move the ones that don't work.

As nutrients wash away every time you water, feeding is important. I use a twenty-twenty-twenty water-soluble fertilizer, one tablespoon (15 milliliters) to a gallon (3.8 liters), once a week. Although this is not a how-to gardening book, these tips are offered because you can't judge the success of a color scheme unless the plants are growing well.

Over time, I have hit upon a design formula for containers. For large pots or tubs, I use from three to five major plants; a tall plant to give the arrangement height; one or two specimens with impressive flowers or bold foliage to carry the color scheme; a filler to round out the composition; and something to trail or billow over the hard rim of the container.

THE RIGHT POT: CHOOSING CONTAINERS

⁓

First of all, you have to decide what part the container will play in the overall scheme of things. Should you feature the pot or the plants?

If you are lucky enough to own an exquisite earthenware vessel with classic lines, the container should take precedence over the plants. It should be given an appropriate setting and allowed to dominate its surroundings.

If, however, the container is pedestrian, it should play second fiddle to the plants and recede courteously into the background.

COMMISSIONING A CONTAINER

One summer, I had an idea that depended on finding a turquoise-blue container. No leaf or flower comes anywhere near that color, and without it, my scheme would completely lose its character. In addition to the right color, the container had to be the right shape. To accommodate the plants I wanted to use, it had to be at least eight inches (20 cm) deep and about three times as wide.

An exhaustive search proved fruitless, and the following spring I presented the problem to Trevor Youngberg. Youngberg is the resident potter at Oliver Nurseries in Fairfield, Connecticut. Although he had never tackled such a large piece before or tried to match a specific color, he was intrigued by the challenge and willing to experiment. In the end, he produced a beautiful turquoise-blue bowl of exactly the right dimensions. You will meet this talented young man again in Chapter 15 and will understand why I went to such lengths to get that bowl.

Any of the low-key, neutral tones found in nature are suitable colors for such containers. On the other hand, the container can play a part or even dictate the color scheme.

TERRA-COTTA POTS

Generally speaking, I belong to the school of thought that puts the plants first and the container second, which is why I like terra-cotta. The soft hues of earthenware go with every color. Terra-cotta literally means "baked earth" and comes from the Latin and Italian words for *cook* and *earth*.

Terra-cotta works well in the garden

because it is naturally earth-toned.

Being of the earth themselves, the fire-born tones of reddish-brown, burnt-orange, and rosy-beige—depending on the mineral content of the clay—blend into the outdoor picture. They take nothing away from the flower colors and provide a subdued but attractive contrast with green leaves.

The most beautiful terra-cotta pots come from Italy and are made by hand, a laborious process that begins with special clays mixed with sand and kneaded into a stiff dough. The dough is stored below ground to cure until the potter pronounces it fit for the wheel. Then it is thrown and shaped, and the pots are allowed to dry before their final trial by fire. In Italy, terra-cotta is considered peasant pottery. But overseas, it is treasured by gardeners for its gentle hues and earthy texture. Being heavy and fragile, it is expensive to transport and, therefore, to buy on this side of the Atlantic.

One of my favorite sights in the fall is the serried ranks of empty terra-cotta containers lined up on the terrace. Empty and yet so full of promise, they stand upright, rim to rim, ready to be put away in the cellar. I never leave my terra-cotta pots outside full of earth in the winter. Being porous, terra-cotta absorbs water. If the moisture freezes and expands, the pottery cracks. Glazed terra-cotta pots are even more susceptible.

Cement's neutral gray enhances the subtle color scheme in Jerry Fritz's Pennsylvania garden.

Alternatives to Terra-Cotta

Plastic and fiberglass pots that look like terra-cotta are sensible alternatives for large plants, like *Brugmansia*. Every summer for the last twelve years, I have grown a pair of *Brugmansia* 'Charles Grimaldi,' one for either side of the glass doors onto the terrace.

By the end of the season, these South American shrubs have reached heights of six feet (1.8 m) or more, and getting them out of their pots takes three of us. To loosen the massive root ball, we have to thump the sides of the pots and roll them around on the ground. No clay pot would stand up to that abuse.

Besides being tougher than clay, the plastic and fiberglass pots are far lighter. They are a godsend when we have to carry plants up our steep, narrow, old-fashioned stairs to their winter home in the spare bedroom. Some of the high-quality plastic and fiberglass pots are even handsome in their own right. And when they are full of plants, it is hard to tell them from the real thing.

Plastic and fiberglass have another advantage. They are flexible enough to give when the soil freezes and are, therefore, winter hardy and don't have to be brought inside. A pair of plastic pots containing little Alberta spruces have been in situ on the terrace wall—summer and winter—for the past three years.

Cement is another material that works well for containers. Heavy but durable, the rough texture and neutral gray color go with all hues, but some grays are more attractive than others. I have read that both cement and terra-cotta can be prematurely "weathered" by painting the sides and rims of the containers with yogurt. The yogurt encourages moss to form, which softens the hues of the material.

Wooden containers are lighter than cement, relatively long lasting, and can be painted any color you fancy to either contrast or harmonize with a particular scheme. Unpainted wood is unobtrusive and works best in our setting. White cedar, which is used for window boxes and planters, turns a pleasant bark gray. Oak whiskey barrels age to brownish-gray, and the rusty steel hoops tone in with the colors of the wood. Oak barrels last up to ten years and can stay out in the winter.

Glazed ceramic containers are relatively fragile but can be very beautiful. There is nothing more elegant than a Chinese storage jar.

Some are so exquisitely decorated that they should be allowed to determine the color scheme. But if you have a combination of colors firmly in mind, don't forget about Youngberg or other local potters..

Although I've never been attracted to cast-off footwear—like sneakers and rubber boots—as flower pots, you can use anything you want, as long as it is suitable for growing plants. This means it must be at least six inches (15 cm) deep and have one or more drainage holes. You can buy porous fiber mats to line standard hanging baskets, and you can even use wicker baskets by lining them with plastic and punching out drainage holes.

There is no such thing as too many containers. I love all kinds, sizes, and shapes and am especially partial to my hens and chicks, which are planted with hens-and-chicks (*Sempervivum*). The reddish-orange tone of the Mexican pottery complements the gray-green of the succulents.

ANNUALS AND TENDER PERENNIALS FOR CONTAINERS

Choosing the Best

CONTAINER COLOR SCHEMES SHOULD BE worked out at a leisurely pace. You have to visit nurseries, study the color range of different plants, and compare colors. This is the moment of truth. At last, you have before you a huge array of living plants in a rainbow of colors. What next?

BEGINNING A COLOR SCHEME

Start assembling your color scheme right there in the nursery. Get a wagon and go up and down the aisles collecting the colors. Then, find an out-of-the-way corner and start putting the plants together, just as you would in the container.

Now, for the questions. You have to ask yourself if this pink geranium goes with this red coleus. To find the answer, put the plants side by side and study them. Bring on more pinks and reds and look again. Shuffle and juggle them until you like what you see. Add the fillers and trailers to your scheme. Does that yellow-green foliage add to or detract from your color scheme? These are not trick questions; they are the only way to train your eye.

What to Look For

When I began gardening, if I wanted anything in the least unusual, I had to grow it from seed or send away for it. Today, the riches of the plant world are available at local garden centers. The temptations are great. There are so many intriguing plants! But for experimenting with color in containers, you need plants that perform certain services.

Container subjects have to bloom long and generously. And their blossoms have to have clout. Plants with intricate forms and subtle colors can be fascinating additions to containers. But

to carry the burden of the color scheme, you need showy flowers and dramatic foliage, or both. These requirements are best met by annuals and tender perennials.

It may take annuals purchased in a six-pack from three weeks to a month to hit their stride. But once established, they will bloom until frost, as long as the spent flowers are removed. Although we routinely call them annuals, many of our most valuable and familiar container plants are tropical or subtropical perennials from Zones 9 and 10. Two of the very best are, for flowers, good old zonal geraniums (*Pelargonium × hortorum*) and, for spectacular foliage, coleus (*Solenostemon scutellarioides*). I single out these two because they have all the qualities needed for successful color experiments: striking good looks, vigorous health, and an extensive color palette.

GERANIUMS

Everyone is familiar with geraniums. Their consistent bloom and bold flower clusters can hold a composition together all summer. Except for white, the range of hues lies in a narrow, essentially warm wedge of the color wheel. Colors include every imaginable red, from magenta to nearly orange, and infinitely graded pinks, from apple-blossom to rose and from salmon to coral. But that's not all; many also have brightly colored foliage.

For foliage, my favorite is 'Crystal Palace Gem.' The centers of the high-intensity chartreuse leaves are stamped with green. Above them, elegant clusters of small, vivid coral flowers open, a few at a time.

COLEUS

~

If geraniums are the perfect flowering plants for containers, coleus are the hands-down winner in the foliage department. Recent hybridizing efforts have produced a scintillating palette of hues and patterns. There are colors to go with every scheme, warm or cool.

Although the patterns of 'Atlas' and 'Solar Flare' contain reds and yellows, both lean toward the cool side of the spectrum and would look best with crimson, lemon yellow, and yellow-green. The yellow-green foliage of 'Enchantment,' embellished with complex maroon veining, goes with both warm and cool hues. The complementary color combination of maroon and yellow-green also appears in 'The Line,' except that maroon is confined to the midrib—hence, the cultivar name. In solid colors, you will find warm reds, like 'Red Quilt'; cool yellow-greens, like 'Golden Wizard'; and dark shades of red and purple that can be either warm or cool.

Although coleus is usually thought of as a shade plant, cultivars with richly colored leaves need at least a few hours of morning sun

LEFT: Coleus also offers a variety of leaf forms and growing habits.

RIGHT: Coleus varieties are perfect for adding colorful foliage to a container scheme.

to bring out the best in them, and most are tolerant of full sun. The typical leaf shape is a pointed oval, toothed around the edge, which gives coleus the common name of "painted nettle." But the so-called duck foot forms have small, lobed leaves that look more like mittens than duck's feet. And the nearly black leaves of 'Inky Fingers' resemble miniature gloves. Plant habit varies from bushy and upright to low and cascading.

Never out of bloom or in need of deadheading, foliage plants, like coleus, provide the stable backdrop that flowering plants need to maintain an enduring color scheme. Their trailing counterparts are useful to carry the color scheme down to the ground.

New varieties of vines bring unusual colors

and shapes to the container garden.

Ipomoea batatas 'Margarita' goes well with warm hues.

Vines

In the old days, you had a choice of two vines for this purpose: ivy or vinca. Now, dozens of interesting vinelike plants are available. *Tradescantia pallida* 'Purple Heart' has jointed stems that grow both upward and downward and are thick with bloomy, deep-purple leaves. The small triangular flowers are mauve-pink, which should give you an idea for at least one suitable color companion.

Black sweet potato vine (*Ipomoea batatas* 'Blackie') became enormously popular a few seasons ago. The long stems grow to perhaps eight feet (2.4 meters), bearing an abundance of eye-catching black leaves shaped like three-lobed maple leaves. 'Blackie' looks gorgeous wandering among red geraniums. Its close relation *Ipomoea batatas* 'Margarita' has shorter vining stems and broader golden-green leaves that go particularly well with warm color schemes.

OTHER STUNNING
FOLIAGE PLANTS

Plectranthus, a close relation of coleus and a relative newcomer to the container scene, was recently described in one of the cutting-edge catalogs as "a hot little genus." It resembles a large, vigorous coleus with well-branched stems and handsome green, gray, or variegated leaves. *Plectranthus forsteri* 'Aureomarginatus' has green leaves broadly edged in yellow, and *forsteri* 'Marginatus' has white-edged green leaves.

The cultivar *Plectranthus fruticosus* 'James' offers a combination of deep-green leaves dramatically veined in purple. The stems match the veining and make a striking contrast to the yellow foliage of Japanese forest grass (*Hakonechloa macra* 'Aureola'). The grass is a perennial that has to be returned to the garden in the fall. But it's worth the trouble because its bright waterfall of foliage does so much for a yellow-purple container scheme.

THIS PAGE: Japanese forest grass in a yellow-purple container scheme.

OPPOSITE, TOP: Red fountain grass provides height and grace. BOTTOM: Cannas offer both handsome foliage and striking flowers.

Plectranthus argentatus, one of the very best, is shown here in a garden setting with another prime foliage plant for pots, annual red fountain grass (*Pennisetum setaceum* 'Rubrum'). The grace and refinement of grasses lighten container compositions that are heavy on foliage and flowers. Red fountain grass has narrow, arching burgundy blades and fuzzy flower heads that go divinely with many of the coleus cultivars that have red leaves.

The energetic thrust of spiky plants gives containers a shot of excitement. I am fond of yuccas and often start off new ones in pot schemes, planting them in the garden in the fall. New Zealand flax (*Phormium*), the Mercedes Benz of spiky plants for containers, appears on pages 219, 220, and 222. Phormiums are not always easy to find and are, alas, expensive. But tender dracaenas are cheap, available, and very useful. Having narrow, flexible green blades that fan out at the tips, they are softer in outline than the yuccas and *Phormium*.

Superior foliage is essential in any container plant, whether it bears flowers or not. Cannas (*Canna* × *generalis*) have both stunning foliage and knock-your-socks-off flowers of red, orange, pink, or yellow. They belong to a tropical genus that grows from a fleshy rootstock that can be stored in the cellar for the winter. The plants are distinguished by their stately proportions and broad, often prominently veined leaves. Variegated forms boast stripes of yellow, pink, orange, or red or a combination of colors; solid leaf colors include shades of green and dark maroon.

Dahlias also receive top marks for foliage, with compound leaves—bronze, dark red, or solid green—that stay attractive all summer. Like daylilies and other popular garden plants, dahlias are the darlings of hybridizers, who have created a staggering 20,000 cultivars. Sizes range from neat "patio" size one-footers to soaring six-footers, with proportional flowers—big plant, big blossom. You can choose from twelve different flower styles: petite balls to daisy shapes to quilled forms the size of butter plates. Although warm colors predominate and include every tint and shade of red, pink, yellow, and orange, there are also cool pinks, lilacs, and purples.

Dahlias divine!

Connecticut gardener Chrissie D'Esopo demonstrates the color range of petunias and impatiens in this wonderful display.

Choosing Hues

In searching through catalogs for flowering annuals to use in container schemes, I made an interesting discovery. The warm side of the spectrum is much better represented than the cool. There are numerous reds, pinks, yellows, and oranges among annuals suitable for containers, like impatiens, petunias, zinnias, and marigolds. But cool hues are in short supply, especially true blues. That is probably why gardeners are so obsessed with blue. Even lavender-blues are less common than tints of mauve. But here are a few suggestions.

In addition to innumerable pinks and magentas, petunias provide many bluish-purple shades. 'Azure Pearl' is blue-violet, and some of the new blue-veined cultivars read from a distance as tints of lavender-blue.

Salvia farinacea 'Victoria,' with narrow, violet-blue flower spikes, and *Salvia farinacea* 'Strata,' with silver stems and calyxes and lighter blue flowers, grow just as well in containers as they do in the garden. And they are among the bluer of the blue tender perennials.

Anagallis monellii, another perennial that behaves like an annual north of Zone 8, comes close to being a true, dark, gentian-blue. And new in my life last year was the delightful, *Evolvulus nuttallianus* 'Hawaiian Blue Eyes.' This is an excellent container plant with a semitrailing habit and small gray-green leaves studded with flat, almost true-blue flowers an inch (2.5 cm) across.

The more familiar and more numerous bluish-violet flowers include *Nierembergia repens*, with fine foliage and cup-shaped blossoms; cultivars of *Browallia* with bell-like flowers; and *Laurentia axillaris*, with masses of dainty, lavender-blue stars.

The glories of blue!

Although lobelias (*Lobelia erinus*) come in beautiful shades and tints of true blue, I have always found them to be willful little plants. After a few weeks of life in a container, mine always seem to go into a decline. But many other gardeners highly recommend this dainty edging plant. 'Crystal Palace' is deep blue, and 'Cambridge Blue' is the color of a summer sky.

With the exception of the lobelia, I have grown all the other plants successfully, some for many years, and can vouch for their good behavior in containers.

8

APPEARANCES

The Way We See Colors in the Garden

WITHOUT QUESTION, ORCHESTRATING colors in the garden is more difficult than creating color schemes in containers. Scale and distance are part of the problem. Even a modest flower bed is much larger than a container. A color scheme that worked in a pot may be too gaudy on a larger scale or the reverse, an interesting container combination may lack impact from a distance.

LIGHT

~

Light is a key issue. Out in the garden, the appearance of color is affected by the amount and quality of the sunlight. Usually, containers are closely associated with the house or even attached to it. And at certain times of day, the building affords a container scheme some protection from the sun. But in the open garden, the colors may not look the same as they did in a window box or on the patio. Heat and sunlight, over which we have almost no control, play a significant role in the appearance of colors.

The two photographs of my September border were taken on the same day during the morning hours between sunrise and eight o'clock. But the colors look different because one picture was taken with the sun out, and the other, when it was behind a cloud. In the golden light of early morning, that brief period called the "magic hour" by photographers, the colors in the border radiated warmth; but the cloud extinguished their glow.

Garden colors look their best at the beginning and the end of the day, especially at the height of the summer season. In the middle of the day when the sun is overhead, even hot, bright colors take a beating. But there is nothing you can do about it, except plant trees. Although shade is flattering to all colors, especially cool, pale hues, the majority of common perennials prefer sun. So, it is a conundrum. If you want to grow sun lovers but can't bear their wan appearance at midday, stay out of the garden at noon.

Hot colors like the red, orange, and yellow of these daylilies hold up much better in bright sunlight than their pastel counterparts.

Fortunately, we can choose colors to suit a particular situation. I've seen for myself how much better red, orange, and yellow daylilies hold up on a hot, sunny day than their pastel counterparts. Although the pastels often fade to beautiful tints, they are nothing like the original hues.

No wonder gardeners in Mexico and the American Southwest display unabashed enthusiasm for bright crayon colors that make the English shudder. The pastels that appear luminous under Britain's overcast skies could never hold their own under the Southwest's fierce onslaught of heat and sun.

The *Agastache* and *Portulaca* blossoms appear to match, but in the garden the small tubular *Agastache* fade behind the *Portulaca*'s larger blooms.

PLANT FORM AND PLANT HABIT

In the garden, structure and plant habit also affect our impression of hues. The size, shape, and number of individual flowers; the configuration of flower clusters; and the texture of petals and leaves all have some bearing on our perception of color.

Matching flower colors but mixing sizes, shapes, and forms shows you how hue can be affected by certain aspects of the plants themselves. Close up, the soft, rosy-orange flowers of *Agastache* 'Apricot Sunrise' exactly match *Portulaca* 'Sundial Mango.' But in the garden, they don't. Of the two, the *Portulaca* seems a brighter and more intense color. Its full, semidouble blossoms, like little roses, face out toward their audience. The dainty tubular blossoms of the *Agastache* hang shyly downward and retreat into a haze of less-intense color.

From a distance, *Veronicastrum virginianum*, with two-dozen or more candelabra-branching stems, hasn't a fraction of the carrying power of half a dozen white lilies (*Lilium longiflorum*). The lily flowers are large—at least seven inches (17.5 cm) long—with sleek lines, a smooth texture, and several flowers to a stem. The flowers of the *Veronicastrum* are countless, but minute, and their emerging stamens give each flower spike a fuzzy outline. The result is that although both plants bear pure white flowers, those of the lilies look whiter. Set off by the *Veronicastrum*'s grayish haze of fine flower spikes, the glamorous lilies seem even more radiant.

On a larger scale, you can see how flower form influences color perception by comparing the blossoms of the native fringe tree (*Chionanthus virginicus*) with those of a hybrid rhododendron. Both have white flowers. The fringe tree's botanical name comes from the Greek

In this pairing at White Flower Farm in Litchfield, Connecticut, both flowers are pure white, but the lilies look whiter because they are larger.

The flower heads of the rhododendron have greater garden impact than those of the fringe tree on the left.

word for *snow*; the rhododendron is a cultivar called 'Boule de Neige'—French for *snowball*. Both shrubs are mature specimens that bloom profusely, but there the similarities end.

The individual blossoms of the fringe tree have four thin petals, less than an eighth of an inch (3.1 mm) wide. They are loosely massed in soft, drooping mops of bloom beneath umbrellas of expanding yellow-green leaves. Sunlight, filtered through the new foliage, colors the flowers chartreuse, creating an effect that is more ethereal than eye-catching.

The rhododendron, which blooms earlier, has impressive flower trusses that would far outshine the fringe tree's mass of delicate flowers if the two plants bloomed at the same time. Instead of wispy

The size and shape of the rhododendron's flowers and its darker green foliage make it stand out more in the garden than the fringe tree.

blossoms in loose panicles, the rhododendron sports relatively large flowers compressed into solid balls of bloom.

The snowballs appear much whiter than the airy panicles of the fringe tree for two reasons: first, the respective sizes, shapes, and forms of the flower clusters; and second, the degree of contrast between the flowers and foliage.

The contrast between the snowy rhododendron trusses and their platforms of dark green leaves is dramatic. The chartreuse-tinted white flowers of the fringe tree almost match the yellow-green foliage.

The shiny surface of the gardenia reflects the light, while the matte surface of the *Plectranthus* leaves (top half) absorbs it.

TEXTURE

～

Although texture affects color in subtler ways than size, shape, and form, the surface quality of petals and leaves does make a difference. The mature foliage of the gardenia in the photograph looks lighter than that of *Plectranthus thyrsoideus*, although the two actually match. It is the shiny surface of the gardenia leaves that makes the difference. It reflects the light, but the matte surface of the *Plectranthus* leaves absorbs it.

In my garden, the band of lamb's ears edging the long border is made up of *Stachys byzantina*, with patches of the cultivar 'Helene von Stein' at each end.

The difference in surface texture also affects these two variations of lamb's ears.

From a distance, there is a noticeable difference in color between the two. Velvety to the touch and covered with dense white surface hairs, the leaves of *Stachys byzantina* appear a bright, silver-gray. The larger leaves of 'Helene von Stein,' which are almost hairless, seem both darker and greener. But only the surface of the foliage exhibits this difference in hue. If you turn the leaves over, the colors are almost identical.

In the garden, and in the words of Sir William Gilbert, from *The Pirates of Penzance,*

Things are seldom what they seem,
Skim milk masquerades as cream.

NATURE'S CHOICE

The Benign Influence of Green

As I'm sure you have discovered, using color effectively in the garden is a challenge. There are so many variables and so much to learn. But Nature is on our side. If she had done nothing except create the color green, gardeners would be forever in her debt. Green was an inspired choice for grass and leaves: for mountainsides and tropical rain forests; for pastures and rice paddies; for the wooded hills of eastern North America; and for the gentle, rolling countryside of southern England.

The first time I visited my English grandmother, I wrote home that I had never seen the color green before. It was June, and my uncle had driven me from Southampton to London. I'll never forget the green of that long, low ridge of hills called the Hog's Back. It was a revelation. The newest, freshest, greenest green in the world, a color that appears to have no blue in it, nor a breath of yellow, just green.

From Asia's rice fields to the English countryside, green is Nature's choice for the living landscape.

TRUE GREEN

The other secondary colors bear a resemblance to their respective parents, but true green appears indivisible. Even Leonardo da Vinci could see no trace of blue or yellow in it and regarded it as one of the primaries.

Nature, too, seems to consider green a primary. It is the predominant color of the natural landscape wherever there is sufficient rainfall. In the northeast, the greens vary from the yellow spring green of deciduous trees to the silver-green of native red cedars

(*Juniperus virginiana*) to the dark forest green of balsam firs (*Abies balsamea*).

In nature, green is the color of life. The green pigment molecules in chlorophyll collect light energy and are essential to the photosynthetic process. Although other pigments also absorb light, green is by far the most important receptor.

When people with normal vision are asked to pick four basic hues, green is always one of them. It is the color that makes fewest demands on the human eye. Red has the longest wavelength, and blue, the shortest. These extremes require the most effort and adjustment. Green's wavelength lies in between.

In every way, it is a middle-of-the-road color that asks little and gives much. It is a color that neither insists on attention, nor shrinks from view; it is just there. Calm, soothing, essential, green goes with every hue under the sun. It is a congenial member of cool color harmonies, a refreshing contrast to warm colors, a peacekeeper among incompatible colors, and a benign influence on all colors. Dark enough to enhance light colors by contrast and light enough to be visible among dark colors, green is the ultimate background color.

Green is also Nature's choice in the northeastern United States.

LAWNS

⁓

Green velvet lawns are one of the glories of an English garden, and they set off perennial borders to perfection. Although New Englanders can't expect to have grass like that, any lawn, as long as it is green, does the job. A patchy lawn can't be helped in a dry summer, but it does spoil the picture, no matter how colorful the flowers are.

A foreground of green lawn and a background of green trees and shrubs are the making of flower beds and perennial borders.

Hedges or foundation plantings of mixed evergreens provide an excellent backdrop. Even tall woodland trees can be brought down to garden level by planting an understory of evergreens. In my garden, background rhododendrons function as a green scaffolding for the perennial borders.

FLOWER BEDS

~

During the daylily season, the greenery in my garden makes the hot colors even more vibrant by contrast. But it also performs its peace-keeping duties by weaving the contrasting flowers together and integrating them into the predominantly green landscape.

Greens unite random colors in an alpine meadow and in a summer cottage garden.

A GREEN GARDEN

Betty Ajay, a garden designer and friend of many years, calls green "the sovereign color of summer." A passionate advocate of green gardens, her own is an oasis of peace and tranquility. When I began gardening, I would not have appreciated the deceptive simplicity of Ajay's garden. Seized as I was with perennial fever, I would have felt cheated by the absence of "color." But I have since come around. Although I could never give up my bright colors and beloved daylilies, I do believe that green is the most important single color in any temperate zone garden.

Green is the secret to all successful color schemes, including nature's own, which are invariably harmonious, despite the random draw of other colors. When have you ever seen clashing hues in the natural landscape? Wildflowers in an alpine meadow don't clash. Nor do the mixed colors in a cottage garden—all thanks to green.

Conifers offer a wide selection of greens.

JUNIPERS AND CYPRESS

The range of greens is enormous. Among conifers alone the variety is astonishing. Besides all the green-greens, there are warm yellow-greens, cool blue-greens, and silver-greens. Junipers (*Juniperus*) offer a palette of predominantly cool blue-greens; the false cypress genus (*Chamaecyparis*) provides more warm tones. Even without looking further, a gardener would find a diverse palette and many different forms within these two genera.

Juniperus squamata 'Blue Star' expands into a low, dense mound of prickly steel-blue needles; *J. horizontalis* 'Bar Harbor' and 'Blue Rug' cover the ground with irregular blue-green carpets; and cultivars of *Juniperus scopulorum* and *Juniperus virginiana* shoot straight

AN EVERGREEN GARDEN

Nancy Britz is so smitten with conifers that she has devoted much of her Massachusetts garden to them. Pines, spruces, and firs form the framework for a series of island beds in which she explores the whole range of forms and colors. Intrigued as much by shape and texture as hue, she juxtaposes cones with globes, mounds with cylinders.

Britz also favors contrasts in color and has chosen as a centerpiece in one planting bright yellow *Chamaecyparis obtusa* 'Crippsii,' with a soft pyramidal form, next to squat blue *Picea pungens* 'Montgomery.' In front of these two, a mound of *Chamaecyparis pisifera* 'Golden Mop' repeats the bright note of 'Crippsii.' The medium greens of *Pinus mugo* 'Valley Cushion' and sea-green *Juniperus procumbens* 'Nana' mediate between the bright, flashy yellow-greens and blue-greens.

upward, creating silver and blue exclamation points in the garden.

With only six species in the genus, false cypresses furnish gardeners with a huge number of cultivars in all sizes, shapes, and different tones of yellow, yellow-green, and old gold to contrast with the blues of the junipers. You have already met two in my garden: *Chamaecyparis pisifera* 'Filifera Aurea,' a large conical shrub with sprays of threadlike golden-green foliage, and *Chamae-cyparis pisifera* 'Filifera Aurea Nana,' a low mounded version with foliage of a more subdued golden-green.

Hostas and ferns are good choices for a shady, green garden.

HERBACEOUS BORDERS

~

For green gardens using herbaceous plants, shade-loving *Hosta* and ferns are winners. Culturally compatible, the two also play to each other's strengths in terms of design. Tall, elegantly divided fern fronds call attention to the imposing bulk of mature *Hosta* clumps; *Hosta* return the favor by making the ferns seem even lighter and more graceful by comparison.

All the common native ferns of eastern North America make ideal *Hosta* companions. The most delicate, maidenhair fern (*Adiantum pedatum*), has dainty, light-green fans held flat at the top of wiry stems. It spreads slowly into patches that make a lacy fore-

Hostas provide a panoply of green in Wesley Rouse's garden.

ground for *Hosta*. Favorites among the tall ferns include medium-green cinnamon fern (*Osmunda cinnamonea*); the similar interrupted fern (*Osmunda claytonia*); and stately, dark-green ostrich fern (*Matteuccia struthiopteris*).

In my day, *Hosta* were either solid green or green and white, and pretty much "one size fits all." Now, they come in all sizes, from tiny cultivars with leaves no bigger than mussel shells to majestic giants that have leaves a foot (30 cm) wide and longer than my forearm. Foliage colors span the yellow-green to blue-green wedge of the color wheel, and leaf shapes and textures offer even more variation.

Although you could create a beautiful green garden using just ferns and a variety of *Hosta*, there are manifold other choices among the foliage plants that flourish in the shade. Fragile-looking fumitory (*Corydalis ochroleuca*) is an ideal addition to a *Hosta* and fern bed. It has extremely pretty light-blue-green foliage, divided again and again into tiny leaflets. The flowers, which are small, white, and half an inch (12.5 mm) long, bloom from March to November, and the foliage never loses its charm.

Handsome, nearly evergreen hellebores are also high on my list for green gardens. Two species in particular exhibit the long-term good looks required: the lenten rose (*Helleborus orientalis*) and the so-called stinking hellebore (*Helleborus foetidus*). The supposed "stink" of the latter is a barely detectable whiff of skunk that escapes if you deliberately crush the foliage and bury your nose in it. Both species have splendid palmate leaves. Those of the lenten rose are a lacquered forest green; those of *Helleborus foetidus*, black-green with a matte finish.

No green garden should be without gingers either. European ginger (*Asarum europaeum*) offers glittering green kidney-shaped leaves. It is a chic little plant, low growing and tidy. Native gingers have dark-green leaves with a soft, matte finish. Those from the southern Appalachians are often attractively mottled with silver. But I am partial to our local ginger (*Asarum canadense*), with its homespun appearance and vigorous plant habit. The leaves are large, plain, heart-shaped, and a rich dark green.

Finally, Solomon's-seal (*Polygonatum biflorum*), a familiar wilding in our woods, enhances any shade planting with medium-green leaves arranged in pairs along arching three-foot (90 cm) stems. Small, bell-shaped white flowers tinged with green hang from the leaf axils in the spring. Its Japanese counterpart, *Polygonatum odoratum thunbergii* 'Variegatum,' much the same in general design, is

LEFT: Stinking helebore with Lenten rose.

CENTER: Native ginger.

RIGHT: Varigated Solomon's Seal from Japan.

dressier, with distinctive reddish-brown stems and pairs of leaves delicately edged in white.

These and many other desirable foliage plants are hardy woodlanders. So, if you have shade, stop wishing for sun, and instead, enjoy the special pleasures of a green garden. Gardens that depend on foliage have the advantage of remaining attractive for months on end and needing less maintenance than most perennial borders. For a cool, restful summer season, think green.

10

GRAY

The Good Neighbor

ON THE COLOR WHEEL, THERE ARE EIGHT grays between black at one end and white at the other, but nature's grays have a thousand faces. Omnipresent in the animal kingdom, gray is worn by untold numbers of birds, mammals, insects, and reptiles. Gray is nature's choice for much of the earth's crust, for mountain peaks and the mists that envelop them, for the bark of trees and the bedrock of New England.

QUALITY OF GRAY

~

Green is a strong presence in the landscape, but gray is a self-effacing hue. It reflects and absorbs a portion of every color. Green, like the other spectral colors, reflects only itself. Green pigment molecules give back the green wavelengths in white light and absorb the rest. The beauty of gray is that it is often tinted with colors that have been incompletely absorbed.

One of the letters collected by W. H. Auden in *Van Gogh: A Self Portrait* (1961), was devoted almost entirely to the color gray. The artist marveled that nature could concoct such "an endless variety of grays—red-gray, yellow-gray, blue-gray, green-gray, orange-gray and violet-gray." Looking around, you will begin to see them,

too—that bit of green in the gray bark and buds of the cup-and-saucer magnolia, the plum cast to the gray-green rosettes of *Sempervivum*.

The number and complexity of nature's grays prompted van Gogh to write: "The colorist is the man who knows at once how to analyze a color, when he sees it in nature, and can say, for instance: That green-gray is yellow with black and blue, etc. In other words, the man who knows how to find nature's grays on his palette."

GRAY IN THE GARDEN

~

Painters have to figure out the component colors to mix these illusive grays. Gardeners have only to welcome them into their gardens as walls, walks, decks, patios, ornaments, and, of course, plants. Grays go with every hue because no single wavelength is dominant. This kindly, unobtrusive, infinitely variable color plays handmaiden to all other hues.

Next to gray, bright colors remain characteristically vivid and pastels glow. Often, the charm of an English border is the combi-

nation of gray foliage plants with flowers in tints and shades of clear blue and pink, misty violet and pale yellow.

Gray also plays an indispensable role in all white gardens. In the most famous, at Sissinghurst Castle, in Kent, England, a memorable weeping pear with silver leaves presides over one end of a crosswalk. Along the walk, silver-gray lamb's ears and various pale-gray artemisias tumble onto the darker gray flagstones.

Gray with dark foliage colors is a classic on both sides of the Atlantic. Dark reds and purples appear darker by contrast but also richer. Nestling in the soft foliage of *Artemisia* 'Silver Mound,' rosettes of *Aeonium* 'Schwarzkopf' look dark and lustrous, with gleams of red at the center of each rosette. The contrast is dramatic, but not as extreme as it would be with white. White would blind the viewer to nuances in the red. Gray allows them to shine through.

In the hills of southwestern Connecticut, exposed slabs of gray bedrock form the ridges that run north and south from the Berkshires to the Appalachians. The rocks along my stream in the woodland garden are chips off the old block. They are stippled black and white, flecked with silver mica, and encrusted with lichens. Next to their rough hides and mellow tones of gray and gray-green, the pale colors of the delicate spring flowers appear even fresher and more fragile.

Over eons, weathered chunks of rock have broken away from the ridges and rolled downhill. In the nineteenth century, farmers cleared

Gray sets off rich, dark colors; enhances bright colors; and flatters pastels.

them from the land and built the miles of stone walls that still pay tribute to their diligence. Along sunny country roads, natural-ized orange daylilies stage a bril-liant show against these haunting remnants of Connecti-cut's past. A background of gray stone enhances all flower colors.

Rock gardeners don't worry about color because nature provides a flattering gray backdrop for their alpine jewels. However, integrating a man-made rock garden into the home landscape isn't easy. It helps to have a naturally rocky site. An exposed ledge can be very effec-tive planted with ground-hug-ging plants, like heathers and heaths. Fractures in the rock provide suitable homes, as long as the soil is deep enough and acid enough.

In their native habitats, alpine plants drive long taproots into cracks and crevices in the mountainsides or creep over the broken rock particles of screes. It doesn't matter that nature has chosen the flower colors arbitrarily

THIS PAGE: Tints and shades of gray rock set off the flowers of heaths and heathers.

OPPOSITE: A gray wall provides a neutral background for colorful pinks and creeping phlox.

or that the hues are vivid and varied. All are well served by the tints and shades of gray rock.

At the Botanic Garden of Smith College, in Northampton, Massachusetts, a stone retaining wall satisfies the cultural requirements of alpine and saxatile plants. Tucked into spaces between the weathered gray rocks, pinks, moss campion, creeping phlox, and other rock lovers look very much at home. The wall not only shows off their bright flowers, but also brings them closer to the viewer.

SHADES OF GRAY

~

In the plant world, grays can be almost as light and reflective as white or as dark as slate. The lamb's ears along the front of my border are at one extreme of the black to white scale; the globe-shaped rosettes of *Agave victoriae reginae* are at the other. In between lie all the soft tones of gray described by van Gogh.

The lamb's ears edging my border are a light, bright gray.

The curious shapes and forms of succulents and cacti exhibit many of these tinted grays in their fleshy foliage. The dark agave in the photograph on page 155 rests on a pale, blue-gray carpet of *Echeveria*. In another grouping of desert plants, the foliage of blue-chalk-sticks (*Senecio serpens*), which truly lives up to its name, surrounds fluted green-gray columns of organ-pipe cactus (*Lemaireocereus marginatus*).

Green-grays in the middle of the value range are among the most versatile of all garden colors. If I had to choose one plant

At Longwood Gardens, the two gray-green rosettes of agave are at the dark end of the gray scale.

to illustrate the virtues of these midgray tones, it would be *Plectranthus argentatus*. The specific name refers to the frosty overlay of silver that turns the leaves green-gray and the stems violet-gray. Although this Australian native is tender in my Zone 6 garden, it is easy to grow from cuttings or plants purchased in the spring. Set out in the garden in late May, even cuttings soon achieve the stature to compete in a perennial border. This *Plectranthus* is also one of my favorite plants for container color schemes.

In my friend Peter Wooster's garden, it holds its own with *Yucca filamentosa* and even woody *Buddleia davidii* 'Pink Delight.' The mauve stems and flower spikes of this paragon supply a missing link between the cool pink blossoms of the *Buddleia* and the purple (*Tradescantia pallida* 'Purple Heart') in the foreground.

In a container scheme featuring its countryman Australian fan flower (*Scaevola aemula*) and magenta petunias, the green-gray leaves enhance the petunias by contrast. At the same time, the violet-gray stems bridge the gap between the intense red-violet of petunia 'Ultra Burgundy' and the fan flower's paler tint of red-violet.

LEFT: The blue-chalksticks highlight the green-gray of the organ-pipe cactus at Longwood Gardens.

RIGHT: Mauve stems of the plectranthus link the cool pink Buddleia blossoms to the purple foliage in the foreground.

Gray acts as a bridge between intense and pale hues.

This is what makes gray foliage so valuable—its ability to bridge differences and create unity and accord.

When gardeners are disappointed in their color schemes, it is often because extreme differences in hue, value, or degrees of intensity have not been reconciled. By providing an infinite range of soft intermediate tones, gray performs wonders as a go-between. Gray, not white, is the great blender.

11

WHITE

Star Quality

IN THE THEATER AND IN PUBLIC LIFE, there are people who command attention simply by being there. They have a special grace and power that draws others to them. Audrey Hepburn had it; Princess Grace and Princess Diana had it. For better or worse, generations of Kennedys have had it, and Katharine Hepburn still has it—that *something* called "star quality." In the landscape and in the garden, white has star quality, the capacity to turn all heads.

Absolute white has no color. It absorbs no other spectral hue but reflects them all equally. Unlike gray, which absorbs parts of all colors, white remains pure. One-on-one, every color

looks its best next to white because, being unadulterated itself, it preserves their integrity. Paired with white, red looks redder; green, greener; blue, bluer; and so forth.

INTERPRETATIONS OF WHITE

Nature uses white on a grand scale and with a lavish hand, filling the boundless summer sky with parades of majestic clouds. In the winter, the same condensed drops of water that made up the summer clouds freeze and descend as snow, transforming the landscape

into what Samuel Taylor Coleridge might call a "miracle of rare device." On a clear day, the whiteness of clouds and snow make the sky look bluer than blue.

White is a climax color. It crowns the summits of mountains and the crests of waves. Iron and steel turn white-hot before they melt. And condensation from jet engines streaks the sky with white contrails. Even symbolically, white is an extreme. In our culture, it represents an extreme of purity and goodness.

Positive feelings about white probably go back to early man's fear of the dark. The first words associated with color were *light* and *dark*. Black and white. In ancient times, light was looked upon as a gift from the gods. Because nights were fraught with danger, daybreak was greeted with relief and gratitude. Thus, white and black seem to have acquired their respective reputations as symbols of good and evil.

WHITE IN THE GARDEN

~

White, in the garden, is the most misunderstood of all colors. Being the lightest and brightest, your eye goes straight to it. This is "star quality" at work. Even when Katharine Hepburn was in her sixties, she could blow younger women off the stage, just by being there. That's what white can do.

In this garden scene, the elegant, white open-work fence sets off the pure, brilliant colors of roses and daylilies to perfection, but without giving an inch itself. Although it takes up far less space than the lavish display of colorful flowers, the fence is the star of the show. No red, however vivid, nor orange, however flaming, can compete with white.

As in life, there is a downside to celebrity in the garden. White is wonderful in a leading role but disruptive as an ensemble player and useless as a peacekeeper among clashing colors.

Conventional wisdom has it that incompatible hues in a garden can be reconciled by separating them with white. But this doesn't make sense, given the magnetism of white and the fact that every other color looks more purely itself next to white.

Colors clash because the differences between them are too great for comfort. The differences can be in hue, color temperature, or value. But the way to restore unity is always the

Scarlet and white are mutually enhancing in Lynden Miller's garden.

same: reduce the differences by incremental steps. The easiest way to do that is by introducing low-intensity tones of gray, green, or some other appropriate foliage color.

White simply exacerbates the problem. It may be bright enough to take your mind off an incompatible color scheme, but it does nothing to forge links between the disparate hues or foster unity in the garden. Instead, it calls attention to both the offending hue and to itself. Misplaced, white has the ability to wreak havoc in a perennial border. But used with discretion, it can also make all other colors look fresh, clean, and vivid. And as you have just seen, with the white fence, it is particularly effective with strong colors.

Red and white together are as cheerful as Christmas candy canes. The two colors can be combined in a straightforward, highly decorative way, using equal amounts of both, or in a more sophisticated way, using one color as an accent. Award-winning designer of public gardens Lynden Miller allows brilliant scarlet wands of *Crocosmia* 'Lucifer' to find their way up through the variegated green and white foliage of a redtwig dogwood, a combination as lively as it is elegant.

Orange can be a difficult color to integrate into the garden. But introduce it to white, and you have a marriage made in heaven. Orange daylilies against a white fence look even better than they do against a fieldstone wall. The gray wall gracefully bows out, allowing the daylilies to shine. But white meets orange head on, and the two colors push each other to the heights of purity and contrast.

Egg-yolk yellow is another strong color that is hard to place. Many gardeners shun the spring-blooming *Kerria japonica* for this reason, and I admit to being one of the shunners until I saw this twiggy shrub, covered with bloom, growing beneath a white dogwood. The dogwood's starched bracts are the perfect contrast with the *Kerria*'s bright blossoms.

Besides being the ideal partner for hot, bright colors, pure white is at its beautiful best with cool hues, especially blue. White with blue has been a popular motif in decoration for centuries and has graced pottery and porcelain from many periods and many countries. It is no less winning in the garden.

LEFT: Even egg-yolk yellow works with white.

RIGHT: Pure white also sets off cool blue to perfection.

DIVERSITY OF WHITES

White ringed with green.

In nature, there are probably thousands of whites that actually contain pigments that reflect other hues. A breath of yellow in a near-white daylily like 'Joan Senior' results in a creamy white; the early blooming flowers of *Helleborus orientalis* display a green tinge; and apple blossoms offer up a pink blush. Tinted whites are easier to incorporate into a border of mixed colors than pure whites. But tinted or pure, the effect depends not only on the quality of the white, but also on the size and shape of the flowers, their number, and placement.

A few blossoms of a large-flowered white clematis, such as 'Marie Boisselot,' will have much more impact than a mass of snow daisies (*Tanacetum niveum*). Even with the addition of sheet-white *Lychnis coronaria* 'Alba,' it would take acres of snow daisies to balance the flower-power of the clematis. The whiteness of the daisies is compromised by the yellow center of each small flower. And the pure white flowers of the *Lychnis* are not big enough or numerous enough to challenge those of the clematis.

Look through this book at the garden scenes. You will notice that white is used sparingly in all, except designer Wesley Rouse's garden. Indeed, peruse any gardening book, and you will find that white is either the raison d'être of a garden scheme or used with restraint. That being said, the Connecticut garden of Pat Miszuk proves the rule.

The Miszuk garden is built on contrast. White is so light and bright that it contrasts with all colors. Next to white, the greens look

A WHITE GARDEN

When Connecticut designer Wesley Rouse of Pine Meadow Gardens visited Sissinghurst Castle fifteen years ago, he was greatly taken with the White Garden. Returning home, he decided to create his own variation, adding blue to the silver, green, and white scheme. The layout of this home-grown masterpiece bears little resemblance to the original.

Sissinghurst's White Garden occupies a flat, rectilinear space divided into quadrants and enclosed by old brick walls; Wesley's white border is bounded by woodland trees and a broad, grassy path. Working with the rolling Connecticut landscape, he allowed the contours of the hillside to influence the shape of the bed and the curving lines of the path.

Within these gentle confines, a great bank of flowers and shrubs thirty feet (9 meters) deep flows upward with the lay of the land. At the back, the taller shrubs rise to meet the trees. In the middle, dwarf spruces—Christmas tree–shaped *Picea pungens* 'Fat Albert' and rounded *Picea pungens* 'Globosa'—provide structure and a season-long touch of blue.

From spring to fall, white-flowered annuals and perennials drift among the conifers, tall grasses, and flowering shrubs. In June and July, spires of delphinium add punctuation marks of blue among masses of snow-white phlox. And in strategically placed pots, *Plumbago auriculata*, a tender shrub from South Africa, contributes clusters of powder-blue flowers all summer.

However, annuals and biennials are responsible for most of the blue accents: *Cynoglossum amabile* and bachelor's buttons in the spring, followed by sky-blue *Salvia uliginosa* later in the season. In the fall, the blues appear sparingly among clouds of dainty white daisies supplied by asters and *Boltonia asteroides*. In the midst of all the white flowers, the green leaves, and gray leaves, a small lead figure of Pan plays his pipes from spring to fall. This is the kind of setting in which white is really at home.

wonderfully green, and the pinks, dazzlingly pink. In addition, green and pink are near complements and, therefore, set each other off, and white boosts the level of all the contrasts.

The great charm of this garden is its brightness and clarity, qualities it owes to the presence of white. And it works. The linking system among the colors has not been achieved through modulating hues with the addition of low intensity tones; it has been achieved through repetition. Pink and white appear throughout, wrapped in the soothing green embrace of the lawn, hedge, and surrounding landscape.

In elite gardening circles, the lure of white has always been strong. During the late forties, it attracted the clever, curmudgeonly William B. Harris and his wife, Jane Grant. At their country home in Litchfield, Connecticut, they turned a mixed border into a white garden. This garden gave rise to the idea of a nursery of only white flowering perennials and shrubs.

Although that idea was abandoned, the nursery became a reality. And the name White Flower Farm was retained. Today, there is still a gorgeous White Garden at the nursery. Such is the power of this colorless color. It deserves the awe and respect it commands. So treat it with care.

BACKGROUND COLORS

They Also Serve Who Only Stand and Wait

IN FRONT OF A NEIGHBORHOOD HOUSE, a fine old blue colonial, flower beds spilling over the granite retaining wall had been getting more colorful and interesting by the year. Finally, intrigued by the wonderful complementary scheme of yellow, gold, and orange flowers against the blue house, I knocked on the door to meet the owners, Richard and Dorethy Mulligan.

Betty Ajay's gray house harmonizes with Nature's restrained palette.

Their daughter, Oona, who is the gardener, told me that her mother must have planted the first black-eyed Susans years ago. "When I started adding more yellow, a neighbor of mine, who is a Realtor said, 'Yellow flowers sell a house.' But I just like yellow flowers because they're friendly and warm. I wanted the other colors to go with them. And that's how I arrived at the color scheme."

Instinctively, Oona had chosen the perfect colors to contrast with the cool blue of the house. But, too often, gardeners pay no attention to the color of the house. Worse still, they assume that, being colorless, white is the best choice for setting off other hues.

The colors of the Connecticut landscape
are predominantly tints, tones, and shades
of green, brown, and gray.

COLOR IN CONTEXT

~

For a designer, the garden is not a series of flower beds and containers; it is a house and everything around it. The garden includes structures and permanent features, such as walkways, terraces, fences, and steps. These elements must fit together as a cohesive whole that functions efficiently and makes sense. Color is treated like any of the other components. It is considered, first and foremost, in relation to all the other pieces of the puzzle.

In Betty Ajay's serene, spacious designs, the colors are limited in number and subordinate to the larger issues of propriety and

DESIGNING AROUND WHITE

The power of white! My friend Betty Ajay advises that not only is white a liability among mixed colors in a flower bed, but it is an unsuitable background color for a garden. In her book, *Betty Ajay's Guide to Home Landscaping*, published in 1970, she writes: "Most owners who are aware of the interdependent relationship between house color and garden color choose white for the house since it does not conflict with any color scheme in the garden. But a white house stands out sharply and does not blend into the landscape."

To give white its due, she also said that if a house had architectural distinction, it *should* stand out. She described a handsome white house surrounded by greenery as "a pearl on green velvet."

The effect of a white house as a background depends on the degree of contrast between the walls and the surrounding colors. The contrast of a pure white house against a green lawn is extreme and startling, white being the brightest color and green being a relatively dark one. A house makes up a large part of the average home landscape, and flower beds comprise a much smaller part, which results in another dramatic contrast. But if you surround a small white house with a large garden full of light-colored flowers, you have a very different situation.

Pennsylvania garden designer Gary Keim did just that. He took a single-story white bungalow with a generous front porch and made it the background for an enchanting cottage garden. The garden competes successfully with the house by enveloping it in clouds of bloom. And the flower colors, being equally light and bright in value, stand up to the white siding. The porch does its bit, too, breaking up the facade of the house. This illustrates the divide-and-conquer method of dealing with white walls: divide large units into smaller ones. Growing vines on white walls accomplishes the same thing. It reduces the visible amount of white to acceptable proportions.

The Ajay house and garden blend seam-
lessly into the surrounding landscape.

unity. Like other artists, Betty has taken her cues from the natural
landscape, and her gardens reflect the source of her inspiration.

As a newcomer to Connecticut in the forties, Betty used to
drive the back roads, taking note of the way Nature used color. She
saw the tender greens of the deciduous trees in spring and the dark
greens of hemlock, pine, and arborvitae; the snowy flowers of dogwoods and the lean white trunks of birches; the gray tones of the
rocky outcrops and old stone walls. It was a landscape of harmo-

Staining our old farmhouse a color called Desert Sand created an ideal background for terrace color schemes.

nious tints and tones of green, gray, tan, and white, enlivened by incidents of bright color.

When it came time to paint the old farmhouse she and her artist husband had just bought, she wanted a color that would fit into this low-key harmony of Nature's. But first, the Ajays did a study of period houses. And they discovered that gray, not white, was one of the commonest house colors at the time theirs was built. However, it was aesthetic considerations, as much as authenticity, that influenced their decision. They chose gray "to approximate the tonal quality of bark and stone and marry the house to the land."

Betty has been happy with their choice for fifty years. "Although green is Nature's primary color choice," she says, "gray and tan are close seconds. We found that the neutral tone of our house blended with Nature's colors in every season." Working on a few jobs with Betty one year was a real eye-opener for me. I learned to look up and around, rather than always down. And this new way of looking changed our home landscape.

My husband and I first saw our house on a beautiful October day. The maple leaves, which had already turned, were falling fast, and the yellow farm house— rather stiff and prim with its windows a bit too close together—stood in a pool of yellow leaves. It was just as Oona Mulligan's Realtor neighbor said. Yellow sold us the house.

As the winter was long that year, we had ample opportunity to see how the yellow house looked in the snow—beautiful. In the spring, it blended with the delicate chartreuse of the maple tassels. And in the summer, it brought sunlight into our clearing in the woods. As far as we were concerned, yellow was the perfect color. But our two-story barn is red, and so is the small tool barn in the backyard.

I had not minded the two colors, as we never seemed to

The Ravenholt house and garden in Seattle, Washington.

see the red and yellow at the same time. But years later, once we had worked our way around the house, replacing the ancient siding, we decided to switch from paint to stain. This gave me an opportunity to rethink the color. Working with Betty had made me much more conscious of color in the mise-en-scène. And after a bit of soul searching, I decided on a color called Desert Sand. Nor have I been sorry. The neutral beige is not as pretty as the yellow, but it works better with the red barns and as a background for the terrace color schemes.

However, looking at the photographs of Reimert and Betty Ravenholt's house and garden in Seattle, Washington, gives me a pang of regret. Their house is yellow, a paler yellow than ours was, but just as welcoming. And the garden, full of the clearest, freshest pinks and yellows imaginable, goes perfectly with the house color.

A big three-story house situated on a small lot is a challenge to any gardener, but Betty Ravenholt has more than risen to the occasion. And *rise* is the right word. The house, which extends dramatically upward, is crowned by steep gables that exaggerate its height. To tie the structure to the ground and break up the facade, she has trained columns of climbing 'America' roses up the walls on either side of the two front doors.

Other space-saving devices that also reduce the amount of visible wall space include espaliered fruit trees and window boxes overflowing with flowers and foliage. But the most cunning ploy was architectural. The Ravenholts added decks at each level of the house. The effect is of a vertical garden with a tall, yellow house in the midst of it. Yellow, pink, and white are repeated throughout the

The neutral tan of our house fits into Nature's winter color scheme of browns, greens, and grays dramatized by the white snow.

beds, containers, and window boxes, and having similar values, they harmonize with each other and with the light, bright house color.

A blue house, a white house, a gray house, a tan house, and a yellow house. As background colors for a garden, all these hues have been made to work either by establishing likenesses or emphasizing contrasts. Oona Mulligan's hot, bright garden contrasts with the cool blue background; Gary Keim's pastels harmonize with the white background; and Betty Ravenholt's carefully controlled color scheme unifies house and garden.

The tan stain also shows off the vivid hues of summer.

Betty Ajay's gray house repeats the color of the tree trunks and local rocks and blends into the landscape. Ours, with its neutral tan stain, shares winter values with bark, stone, and grasses. In the summer, it shows off the vivid flower hues on the terrace by not competing with them. And that is what background colors are supposed to do.

13

CHOICES

Limiting the Means

IN THEORY, AT LEAST, YOU NOW HAVE ENOUGH information about color to make a beautiful garden. You are familiar with the color wheel and know how to use harmony and contrast; you are prepared to treat white with care and are convinced of the importance of background hues. You have practiced putting color schemes together in containers, and you have accumulated a notebook full of ideas. Now what?

Peter Wooster's garden.

DECISIONS, DECISIONS

~

No gardener I know has ever found a foolproof recipe for using color in the garden. There are as many ways as there are gardeners and so many colors that it boggles the mind. It all boils down to choices. You have to decide how much color and how many different colors you want to use and how you will organize them.

Will you try to manage a great variety of hues, tints, and tones the way Peter Wooster has, within a grid of green velvet lawn? The pure, austere lines of his beds create a framework that controls the wildness within. And an abundance of subtle foliage tones knits all the colors into a rich, complex harmony.

Or are you more like Kathy Loomis, who loves bright, lively colors, and the more the merrier? She relies on her garden's spacious green surroundings to create unity and uses the repetition of key colors to forge the many into a pleasing whole. Or perhaps you relish the peace and serenity of a monochromatic scheme and feel, as Ragna Goddard does, that "Green stands on its own very nicely." Her gardens are orderly, green "rooms" with an architectural quality and a sense of safety and enclosure.

Although Betty Ajay shares Goddard's enthusiasm for green, her gardens have a more expansive feeling and open views that extend outward into the surrounding landscape. Behind her house, smooth green turf, punctuated only by the trunks of canoe birches, sweeps up the hill to meet the woodland

Kathy Loomis's garden.

edge. In the summer, the swimming pool reflects the birches' white trunks.

Once I remarked to Betty that I wanted a garden full of color and excitement. She laughed and said she would rather have a life full of color and excitement and a peaceful garden. She has had both—an intensely interesting life and a green and white garden where tranquility reigns.

Richard Copeland chose a different approach to color but one that also results in a sense of peace and order. He confined fully saturated flower hues to a narrow, harmonious range and provided them with a strong, green framework of hedges.

Ragna Goddard's green "rooms" have an architectural quality.

The elegant simplicity of Betty Ajay's green garden.

In Raymond Hagel's garden, Connecticut landscape designer Mike Donnally has exercised similar restraint, limiting his palette to tonal harmonies with touches of pure color. A subtly varied background of evergreen and deciduous shrubs sets the stage for dramatic accents of brightly painted furniture and displays of seasonal bloom.

Each of these gardeners has arrived at a satisfying arrangement of colors by making choices and imposing restrictions. In an article he wrote in 1917 for the magazine, *Nord-Sud*, French cubist painter Georges Braque maintained that limiting the means gives "an impulse to creation." At the very least, making choices and

THIS PAGE: Raymond Hagel's garden accented by bright furniture and seasonal blooms.

OPPOSITE: Richard Copeland's garden.

exercising restraint limits the opportunities to go wrong. Limitations make your life easier and your garden more effective.

COLOR THROUGH
THE SEASONS

~

In resisting the temptation to use every color under the sun, I have exercised a modicum of restraint. And the sharp edges of the curving garden beds maintain order. Even a naturalistic garden like mine is a far cry from wilderness because the gardener draws lines that proclaim it a work of man.

Of course, all gardens are a collaborative effort between man and nature. And mine is aimed at creating a few periods of peak bloom that fit in with the seasonal colors of the landscape. It is one way of setting limits without sacrificing variety.

Here's how it works. Pastels and other pale colors are particularly appropriate choices for early spring gardens because

The pastels of spring.

Nature can guide a gardener's color palette through the seasons, beginning with spring.

they are in accord with nature's seasonal palette. In April, the background colors are light, bright, and fresh. The sky is China blue, and the trees, yellow-green. To these delicate hues, native shrubs and wildflowers add their tints and shades of yellow, pink, white, blue, and violet. In the garden, our weeping cherry rains down its shower of pink blossoms, and the perennials begin to stir. In the long border, white and cream tulips and narcissus bloom with the emerging foliage of the peonies, irises, and daylilies.

May and June are the frosting months—all pink and white. The woods of Connecticut are laced with white dogwood, followed by a pink-and-white understory of mountain laurel (*Kalmia latifolia*). At the same time, stream banks in sunny, open meadows boast stands of blue flag iris. Pink, white, and blue. In the garden, you can't go wrong with nature's spring classic. From mid-May until early June, my border goes through its red, pink, and blue phase. The pink rhododendrons 'Scintillation' and 'Roseum Elegans,' pale pink 'Janet Blair,' and red 'America' provide the background for red and pink peonies and Siberian irises in shades of blue and violet.

As summer approaches, and the sun rides higher in the sky, its heat and power increase. In the fields and along roadsides, plants like butterfly weed, sunflowers, black-eyed Susans, goldenrod, and New York ironweed fight back with masses of strong color. You

OPPOSITE, TOP: Nature's pinks, whites, and greens. BOTTOM: The early summer border in similar colors.

have to meet force with force. So red, orange, yellow, purple, and gold make good choices for a sunny summer border.

In July, I have the hot daylily colors, and in August, native field and prairie flowers and their cultivars. At the back of the border, giant ironweed *Vernonia altissima* keeps company with *Eupatorium* 'Bartered Bride,' a towering ten-footer (over three meters), and next to the bride, her fancy relation, the gorgeous English selection of *Eupatorium purpureum* 'Gateway.' In front of 'Gateway,' there is shorter New York ironweed and bushy three-foot (90 cm) yellow *Rudbeckia trilobum*.

Entering September, the ornamental grasses begin to produce flower heads in tones of red and purple, and *Sedum* 'Autumn Joy' undergoes its autumnal metamorphosis from pink to rose to russet. At each season, the key colors in the border fit in with those of the natural landscape.

In the fall, the sun rises later, sets earlier, and mellows to amber. As September progresses, many of the summer-flowering plants continue to bloom, blending in with the autumn yellows, reds, and golds. At the end of the month, the foliage season begins in earnest with a burst of vivid color. First, the yellows and reds and golds and oranges; and finally, the leather reds, russets, and old golds. These are also the rich colors of late-blooming mums, which add so much to the fall garden.

Thus, the growing season ends in glory before sinking gently into winter. But winter has its own color palette. In southwestern Connecticut, the deciduous forest subsides into a harmonious quartet of brown, beige, gray, and black, with grace notes of red berries and evergreen accents. Farther north, evergreens dominate the landscape.

A classic winter color palette.

OPPOSITE, TOP: Fall foliage and late-blooming mums. BOTTOM: Early autumn in my border.

LET NATURE SET LIMITS FOR YOU

~

When Betty Ajay and I talk about nature's palette, our references are tied to the local landscape. But desert gardeners speak a different language. Where summer heat is intense and rainfall scarce, green is largely missing.

Landscape colors in Mexico and the Southwest are very different from ours. So are the house colors. The building material of choice is often adobe. Left natural, its warm, earthy hue is perfect with the strong hot colors, which are the order of the day in wildflowers, gardens, and exterior decoration. It takes potent hues to stand up to the desert sun.

Foliage in the desert is sparse or absent altogether. Cacti protect themselves from the sun and heat with hairs, bristles, or waxy coatings that dim the underlying green of their stout forms. And these grayed greens are beautiful against the terra-cotta earth.

Although Nature's choice of background colors is always exemplary, her use of bright colors is also worth studying. Flamboyant displays are brief in duration. Spring bloom in the desert and

New England's fall foliage come once a year and last only a few weeks. It is part of their charm. But on a daily basis, too much intense color would be wearing. And Nature seems to know that.

She reserves her brightest hues for accents: the plumage of birds; the flowers, fruits, and foliage of plants. Against the lower-intensity tones of the landscape, these bright spots stand out.

The least colorful season in the New England year is, of course, winter. At this time of year, the red plumage of a single cardinal glows like a spark against the muted grays, browns, and greens. Perched in a pine or among the dark leaves of a rhododendron, one bright bird has an impact out of all proportion to its size.

Nature uses low-intensity backgrounds to accent spots of bright color.

COLORS IN WINTER

Kenneth Twombly, of Twombly Nursery, in Monroe, Connecticut, knows all about the winter landscape in northern New England. He grew up on a dairy farm in Vermont. The surrounding hillsides were covered with stands of maples and conifers, and he fell in love with trees. In pursuit of his love, he came south to the University of Connecticut to study arboriculture and stayed on to plant trees. Soon, he had twenty-five acres devoted to unusual woody plants and the foundation of a nursery.

Without question, woody plants are the stars of the winter landscape. Even the native shrubs and trees offer beautiful silhouettes and branching patterns and those muted tones of green, gray, black, and brown. But Ken had a better idea: a winter garden featuring both native and exotic trees and shrubs to bring additional color and interest to the winter picture.

I am lucky enough to live near Twombly Nursery and have watched the development of Ken's winter garden with interest and admiration. He started planting in 1994. Against a background of mature conifers and rhododendrons, he sculpted a landscape of hills and dales with a rocky stream running through them.

On the stream banks and knolls and in the valleys, artful arrangements of shrubs and trees with bright stems and bark appeared in front of dark evergreens. At natural focal points in the landscape, he planted golden conifers in groups with their green partners. Elsewhere, red berries glow against evergreen backgrounds.

"It's not like gardening in the summer, when you can use subtle foliage effects or gentle color groupings," says Ken. "The key to winter gardening is contrast." His accent color of choice is yellow to light up a gray day and stand out in contrast to the deep greens and blue-greens of the pine and spruce.

In the garden, less is more, too. You can see how a handful of vivid red dahlias in Helen Bodian's garden grabs the lion's share of attention from the low-key red foliage plants. Although the intense reds are fewer in number, they are the more telling for their relative scarcity. A color accent lends emphasis, not by virtue of its size, but in contrast to the hues surrounding it.

Although gardeners err on the side of too much variety in their flower beds, Nature practices moderation in hers. In *Colour Schemes for the Flower Garden*, the inimitable Gertrude Jekyll, an astute observer of the natural landscape, cautioned gardeners to "plant as Nature plants, with not many different things at a time."

In an alpine meadow, the predominant species are sedges and grasses, interspersed with a few kinds of vigorous field flowers. The grasslike plants create a green background for the flowers, which grow in loose "drifts," a term Jekyll coined to describe groups of like flowers growing in long, thin, overlapping ribbons.

In my woodland garden, I have simply followed Jekyll's advice and Nature's lead. Nature provided the trees, the understory of spicebush, and some of the herbaceous plants: ferns, Dutchman's britches (*Dicentra cucullaria*), and jack-in-the-pulpits (*Arisaema triphyllum*). To these, I have added other native wildflowers and primroses (*Primula*) from Europe and Japan. At home, most of these

Vivid red dahlias stand out among the deep, low-intensity reds of the foliage plants.

Yellows in an alpine meadow and in my
woodland garden.

primroses are wild species, not cultivars, which is why they look natural here among the indigenous woodlanders.

All the flowers are planted according to Nature's own recipe: drifts and not too many different kinds in bloom at the same time. And the color scheme is based on her choice of spring hues. Against the tobacco-brown tones of last year's leaves, the light, bright colors look radiant in the spring sunlight.

THE MAGIC NUMBER THREE

Another Way to Limit the Means

READING THE LANDSCAPE and taking your cue from nature is one way of choosing a palette, but you can also go back to the color wheel for ideas. For garden schemes, three colors seems to be the magic number. Two or three hues, with all their tints, tones, and shades—give or take green—allow ample rein for the imagination without risking anarchy.

TRIAD COMPOSITIONS

~

As you may recall, three colors equally spaced from each other on the color wheel are called a triad. The hues can be as close as one color apart, like red, orange, and yellow, or as far apart as the primaries, red, blue, and yellow. The primaries are separated from each other by three colors, which is almost as far apart as colors can get.

Primary Triads: Red-Yellow-Blue

A composition based on the primaries used at full strength, in equal proportions, and without benefit of greenery is guaranteed to make a strong impression. A primary triad of massed annuals at Hollandia Nursery stops customers in their tracks, which is the intention. But this much bold contrast would soon wear out its welcome in the home garden. On the other hand, reduce the fully saturated colors to tints, add abundant green foliage and you have Ruth Levitan's fresh, sparkling spring color scheme.

Ruth and Jim Levitan's Connecticut garden shows what can be done with the primary triad. White also plays an important seasonal role in this dream of loveliness. Beneath the lacy canopy of white dogwoods, a grass path wanders through seas of forget-me-nots and

pink tulips. On either side, the blue waves lap at the boles of trees and at the feet of red and pink azaleas. My first impression was of flowers everywhere—underfoot, overhead, and on all sides.

In the shady part of the garden, the colors are confined to tints of the primaries. Early in the season, small pale-yellow Tazetta nar-

LEFT: Bleeding heart and pink tulips are
the Levitan's favorites for shade.

RIGHT: In the sunny part of the garden,
the primary colors look fresh and bright.

cissus push up through the carpet of forget-me-nots, followed in May by the pink tulips. Ruth claims that the woodland site dictated the color scheme.

"We bought the property because of the dogwoods," she says. "And I loved blue, so I began planting forget-me-nots and Jacob's ladder. Both do well in the shade." The bleeding heart came from her mother-in-law's garden and inspired the addition of the pink tulips. Meanwhile, her husband, Jim, became interested in rhododendrons and azaleas, which have pink, white, and red flowers. Little by little, the scheme just came together.

At the sunny end of the garden, red, yellow, and blue are used at full strength, but with discretion. Against the green of the emerging daylily foliage, a sprinkling of lipstick-red and buttercup yellow tulips add bright accents. In July, you wouldn't recognize this part of the garden. It is ablaze with daylilies.

Ruth and I both like our daylilies hot. But about ten years ago, I succumbed to some of the newer pinks, which became my excuse for two new flower beds. Although hybridizers are always striving for pure, clear pinks, I love the tints and shades of peach, salmon, and coral that grace my garden. I've combined them with warm,

In July, warm pink and yellow daylilies and blue-violet balloon flowers bloom in Lynden Miller's garden.

golden yellows and a bit of blue-violet for contrast—a warm version of the primary triad.

In painter and public-garden designer Lynden Miller's Connecticut garden, a similar scheme involving daylilies found a home beyond the yew hedge. Through one of the openings, a grass path leads down an allée of crabapples to a garden bench. The crabapples are underplanted with warm pink and yellow daylilies and blue-violet balloon flowers (*Platycodon grandiflora*).

If you like the pink, yellow, and blue combination, there are all sorts of annuals that come in these colors and bloom all summer. The same color scheme could even be carried into the fall with a last hurrah of pink and yellow mums and spikes of blue monk's hood.

THIS PAGE: Red, orange, and yellow are Nature's choices for fall.

OPPOSITE: The same colors are used in Joe Keeler's Garden of Ideas.

Red-Orange-Yellow

In color schemes using three hues separated by only one color, those at each end are far enough apart to be different, but the middle color forges a link between them. Take red, orange, and yellow, for instance: red and yellow have nothing in common, but together they produce orange, which makes them a family.

I love this triad. For summer, there are dozens of annuals that come in red, orange, and yellow, to say nothing of daylilies and other summer-blooming perennials. But these colors have fall written all over them. As they are Nature's own choice for autumn, she has provided plenty of shrubs with colorful foliage, as well as late-blooming perennials in compatible shades, tints, and tones.

Blue-Green-Yellow

Blue, green, and yellow have the same relationship to each other as red, orange, and yellow. But the contrast between blue and yellow is more extreme than between red and yellow because it involves value as well as hue. Blue is the darkest hue, and yellow, the lightest. Joined in wedlock, however, blue and yellow produce green, bringing them together in one of the most satisfying and versatile of color schemes.

In the spring, the acid yellow bracts of cushion spurge (*Euphorbia polychroma*) stand out in striking contrast to the little dark-blue flowers of grape hyacinth. The spurge's green foliage, less bright than the bracts but not as dark as the hyacinths, unites the disparate colors.

The same three hues look very different in a June display at Westpark, a public park in

Munich, Germany. Blue-violet and green play the leading roles; yellow, a small but crucial bit part. Lofty spires of butter-yellow *Verbascum* and tiers of pale-yellow *Phlomis russeliana* pierce the greenery and furnish accents. In both color and plant habit, their spiky forms contrast with the giant clumps of lavender (*Lavendula angustifolia*).

As a garden scheme, the blue, green, and yellow triad has it all. Related by green to its surroundings, it has blue to cool fantastic

The blue-green-yellow triad can be expressed in many forms.

summer's heat and yellow to give it light and life. It is suitable for any garden and any season, including winter, when conifers can be counted on to supply the three colors.

My evergreen garden has given me pleasure for more than three decades, year in and year out. Even when the conifers were young they looked attractive together. Now, they form an impressive frieze of green, chartreuse, old gold, and gray-blue.

GOOD COMPANY

How would you describe a color scheme made up of red, yellow, and yellow-green? It isn't a triad. Red and yellow are three hues apart; yellow-green lies right next to its yellow parent. So it isn't a split-complementary either, although yellow-green is almost directly across from red. Call it what you will, dark red combined with yellow and yellow-green never fail to attract attention in the garden.

It is a win-win color scheme that combines both contrast and harmony. Yellow and yellow-green create harmony, and the extreme value contrast between dark red and bright yellow emphasizes the intrinsic difference between these

two hues. In one garden, a standoff between plum-red *Heuchera*, bright-yellow tulips, and acid yellow-green *Lamium maculatum* 'Aureum' creates high drama. In another, a rich, mellow harmony is achieved by toning down the reds, yellows, and yellow-greens and using more green.

Blue-Yellow-White

White does not appear among the hues around the rim of the color wheel because, technically speaking, it is not a color. So blue, yellow, and white can't be called a triad. But they can certainly be called a trio. A *trio* is a harmonious composition for three voices. And these three colors are made for each other. Although I have no higher authority for this notion, I believe I know why.

Blue and yellow together behave exactly like complements. Yellow emphasizes blue's blueness, making it seem stronger. At the same time, yellow is bright enough to measure up to white. Thus, in combination, the blue is bluer; yellow competes successfully with white; white flatters the other two colors; and together, they make sweet music.

In her sumptuous book, *Tricia Guild On Color*, Guild, an interior designer, describes these hues as "the colors of sunny summer days." Bright sun, white clouds, blue sky. Claude Monet chose the same hues for a dinner service he commissioned for the yellow dining room at Giverny. In the out-of-doors, they were designer Gary Keim's choice for a summer garden in Pennsylvania: blue bachelor's buttons, pale-yellow evening primroses, and soft masses of snow daisies.

For a spring or early summer garden, blue, yellow, and white are perfect colors. Although there are plenty of ways to carry this scheme throughout the season, the yellow flowers of late summer are brassier than those of spring. And the warmer, richer yellows

A spring display at the New York Botanical Garden.

upset the delicate balance of hues. Blue and white are cool colors. Therefore, in the interest of harmony, a cool light yellow is preferable to a yellow that leans toward orange.

Pink-Yellow-White

Another trio, of pink, yellow, and white greets spring with bulbs and fruit blossoms, and the popular trio of pink, blue, and white serenades the month of June with roses and delphiniums. These trios pairing tints of two primaries with white have universal appeal.

These were the colors I loved most when I began gardening. They were the colors of my aunt's garden in England, where the back of the house was smothered in roses and clematis and great stands of delphinium rose higher than the high garden wall. But an overgrown cow pasture is no place for aristocrats of the garden. Ultimately, I pledged allegiance to tough, dependable daylilies and the triad of red, orange, and yellow. After all, you can't have everything.

BORROWING COLOR SCHEMES

The Sincerest Form of Flattery

AT THIS POINT, YOU KNOW EVERYTHING I can tell you about color in the garden. You have all the tools you need to go your own way, which is the only way to go, and I wish you bon voyage.

No matter at what stage you find yourself in this colorful, exciting journey, there is always more to learn. You can go on learning about color for a lifetime and still make new discoveries, as I have. And some of the most recent discoveries have been the most interesting—I have saved them up as a farewell present.

Gauguin, *Parau Parau*, 1892.

As you know, gardening for me has always been about painting, which must mean I am a frustrated artist. In any case, I am a great admirer of the real thing. One day, paying homage to the nineteenth-century French painters at the Yale University Art Gallery, I fell in love with a painting by Paul Gauguin. Standing in front of *Parau Parau*, it suddenly occurred to me what fun it would be to try to copy the colors in plant material.

Parau Parau in a pot: Geraniums, *Salvia splendens*, *Phormium*, and *Helichrysum*.

From that moment on, I was off and running. I bought a slide of the painting and sallied forth to the nearest nursery. I found the warm red in geraniums, the pinkish tangerine in *Salvia splendens*, the salmon pink in the blades of *Phormium* 'Maori Sunrise,' and the foreground tint of yellow-green in the pale foliage of *Helichrysum* 'Limelight.'

The touches of turquoise-blue in the painting indicated a container scheme. That was when I turned to potter Trevor Youngberg (*see* page 100). And now you know why I had to have that blue-green bowl.

MATCHING PLANTS TO FABRIC

The success of the Gauguin scheme inspired more experiments involving the work of artists and designers. The next year, the source of inspiration was a beautiful piece of fabric. I had bought four battered but elegant secondhand metal chairs and a glass-topped table for the terrace, and the chairs needed cushions.

After hours of happily browsing among floor-to-ceiling bolts of fabric at a home-decorating shop, I found a piece of material that

I loved. It was a smooth, tightly woven cotton duck with an all-over pattern of tropical birds, flowers, and foliage. The tropical theme was particularly appealing because I had a cellar full of canna tubers and half a dozen Brugmansia cuttings waiting to be potted. Blue parrots would look right at home among the tender perennials.

Besides blue, the dominant colors were blue-green, dusty salmon pink, and a soft tint of yellow-orange. The Gauguin bowl would fit right in with this new scheme: the trumpets of *Brugmansia* 'Charles Grimaldi' would match the tint of yellow-orange, and the salmon-pink streaks in the *Phormium* I had wintered over were similar to the pink in the material.

I knew that blue would be the stumbling block. The amount of blue in the fabric is substantial, and finding blue-flowered plants suitable for containers is not easy. But a coat of blue paint on the new table and chairs did the trick.

With that problem solved, I set off with one of the cushions to find plants. Matching plant material to a piece of man-made fabric

A piece of fabric inspires a container garden.

is an inexact science. The texture of fabric in no way resembles that of living flowers and leaves. Nevertheless, making color comparisons is an interesting challenge and good eye training. The more you do it, the better you get at it.

I matched the pinks with geraniums, as they have the necessary carrying power. The two cultivars that came closest to the soft, dusty pink in the material were 'Patriot Salmon Blush' and

deeper-salmon 'Schoene Helena.' These I planted in the blue-green bowl, together with the *Phormium*.

In the end, blue-green played a lesser part in the terrace color scheme than in the fabric, but green assumed an infinitely greater role. I also increased the relative amounts of warm colors.

A strain of *Portulaca* called 'Sundial Fruit' had all the right peach, mango, and cantaloupe tints to harmonize with the colors in the fabric. And *Gerbera* daisies offered deeper shades of the same colors.

This harmonious fruit-flavored scheme seemed to need a jolt of more intense color, which gave me the opportunity to use 'Tropicana,' a new canna cultivar. The leaves are a deep, warm red, with translucent stripes of flame and orange. Although these rich tones

THIS PAGE: The fabric-inspired garden came together plant by plant: geraniums in dusty and salmon pinks, then portulaca and gerbera daisies in pastel tints of pink and orange.

OPPOSITE: Canna 'Tropicana' added stronger hues and deeper tones within the same color family.

are not present in the fabric, they belong to the same color family.

The designer of the fabric might not recognize his or her handiwork in this garden interpretation, but it remained true to the spirit, if not the letter, of the design.

I had such a good time adapting the tropical print to plant material that even before the season was over, I had picked out a piece of fabric for the next year.

THE LOVE FOR THREE ORANGES

It was love at first sight. Like the title of Sergei Prokofiev's comic opera, the loosely woven plaid contained three oranges—vivid red-orange, orange, and golden-orange—combined with touches of mauve, two tones of crushed raspberry, and shocking pink. I could hardly wait to start looking for plants to carry out this bold scheme.

To better understand the color relationships in the material, I pulled it apart and separated the colors into skeins. I was not surprised that, collectively, the amount of orange was far greater than any other color. But what did surprise me was that, from a distance, the tones of crushed raspberry looked exactly the same color as the mauve. And when I draped the fabric over the blue table, all the colors with any blue in them seemed to match the table!

Simultaneous Contrast

I was witnessing the effect of "simultaneous contrast." It was fascinating to see in action an optical illusion I had read about but never observed in real life. Here, the predominantly orange stripes in the fabric were casting a blue afterimage over adjacent stripes of mauve and crushed raspberry, making them appear bluer. For simultaneous contrast to work, the colors must remain in a fixed position, which is why this optical illusion can more easily be observed in textiles and paintings than in the garden.

Everything in a garden is in a state of flux. Green leaves intervene between adjacent colors. The positions of the colors change with every breath of wind; buds open and blossoms fall; the sun moves across the sky and passes behind clouds. No, color relationships in the garden are not the same as color relationships in thread or paint.

During the winter, I studied the material and made notes in my color notebook: "Have designs on this new fabric for next summer. For the big matching pots on either side of two entrances, I'm hoping to try a new geranium called 'Tango Orange.' It looks as if it would be a perfect match for the red-orange in the material.

"There is also a new cultivar of Mexican flame vine. The catalog from Logee's Greenhouses makes *Senecio confusus* 'Sao Paolo' sound irresistible: 'The color caught in the daisylike flowers of this vigorous-growing vine is nothing short of a perpetual sunset.' For a filler, zinnia 'Profusion Orange,' a new cultivar of *Zinnia angustifolia*. To go with the mauve stripe, *Browallia speciosa*, and for the shocking pink, petunias."

OPPOSITE: Finding flowers and foliage to match the colors in this fabric was an eye-opening experience.

My projected color scheme underwent many revisions that summer. In Connecticut, it was a phenomenal year for moisture-loving plants. In the garden, the daylilies rejoiced. But the lamb's ears rotted. On the terrace, cannas and *Brugmansia* reached unheard of heights, geraniums sulked, and I never did find the 'Tango Orange.' However, I was able to use "Non-stop" tuberous begonias instead. They loved the wet weather and came in all the right oranges. For impressive foliage and large flowers, I turned to cannas and dahlias. A vivid red-orange canna with green leaves filled the southwest corner with color, and for the opposite corner, 'Tropicana,' from the year before, rose to the occasion with its deep foliage tones and pure orange blossoms.

These colors don't appear in the fabric but the red dahlia works by virtue of its warm bias; the purple tradescantia because it is in the mauve family.

Dahlia × 'Bishop of Llandaff' has single, vivid red flowers with orange sympathies, which made it suitable for this suite in the key of orange. And the very dark red foliage added a deeper note in the right shade. A strain of related dahlias called the 'Bishop's Children' contributed various tints of orange, along with valuable bronze leaves.

But the stars of the show were the tuberous begonias! 'Non-stop Orange,' 'Non-stop Apricot,' and 'Non-stop Flame' lived up to their names, producing flush after flush of spectacular flowers like double hollyhocks.

I didn't use *Browallia* for the mauve component in the color scheme. The trailing habit of Australian fan flower (*Scaevola aemula*) seemed a better choice. And instead of petunias, I tried million bells, *Calibrachoa* 'Trailing Pink,' a suitably "shocking" magenta-pink.

Assembling the cast for this terrace color scheme took several weeks of visiting nurseries. I decided to use only the highly visible colors in the material: the three orange hues, mauve, and a little bit of magenta. I also decided to stick with the designer's proportions of pure orange, red-orange, and golden-orange. But not for long. I had trouble finding the right golden-orange and, in the end, used equal amounts of pure orange and red-orange.

I soon made another interesting discovery. When most of the plants had been planted, I ran upstairs so that I could look down on my handiwork. I had been feeling quite smug about how closely I had managed to match the plant material to the fabric colors. But I was dismayed by what I saw from my office window.

The cacophony of orange and green below came perilously close to strident. Green and red-orange are virtually complements. And each was making the other more vivid and highly contrast-

The begonia 'Non-stop Orange' was the star of the show.

Warm, low-intensity foliage tones unified the whole scheme.

ing. Although I had not anticipated the intensity of that contrast, I did know what to do about it. The solution was to find lower-intensity tones of both colors. Coleus 'Rustic Orange'—and lots of it—came to the rescue, and to tone down the green, masses of yellow-green sweet potato vine (*Ipomoea batatas* 'Margarita'). The warm, low-intensity tones of the coleus and the sweet potato vine wove the entire color scheme together, and it was wonderful.

In fact, nothing I have done in the garden in years has given me as much pleasure as the terrace did that summer. I could hardly wait to wake up in the morning and look out of our bedroom window. When I was working in my office, not an hour went by that I didn't look down on the brilliant array of closely coordinated colors. Even my husband, who doesn't often notice colors, loved the terrace.

And the truth is that I could never have pulled off that scheme if I had not had a nodding acquaintance with color theory. That, and a good eye, is all you need. And both are within reach of any determined gardener.

THE LAST WORD

Conclusions about Color for Gardeners

EVERY BOOK TELLS A STORY. This one began with my rediscovery of the color wheel fifteen years ago. But the seeds were planted in childhood, when a passion for color was nurtured by teachers at my first school. If Robert Fulghum learned all he needed to know in kindergarten, I learned most of life's important lessons between the ages of six and ten at the Country Day School in Watertown, Connecticut.

At this remarkable school, we produced our own plays and wrote stories and poems. We built houses out of packing crates, made blotting paper, and painted up a storm. I still have a progress report from my art teacher, that says I paid "much more attention to line, color, and detail than do most eight-year-olds."

I thought of this the other day when I was at the Metropolitan Museum of Art in New York City. It was a Wednesday afternoon, and the museum was full of children. They sat, lay, and knelt on the floor, like a bright patchwork quilt, copying a Monet landscape. Each child had a pad of paper and a ziploc bag full of colored pencils. Happy and noisy but absorbed, they colored away.

These children were learning to look, and that's what it's all about in painting and gardening. Although I became a far better gardener than painter, I continued to study painting on and off for years and have recently begun to experiment with a new medium, pastels. If gardening has revived my interested in art, art has very much influenced my way of gardening.

The Gardener's Palette is the culmination of what I have learned about color in the garden over a period of many years. It is also the latest chapter in my continuing education. In the summer of 1999, as part of my research, I enrolled in a four day studio workshop that explored the color theories of artist Josef Albers. Albers was a man after my own heart. He believed that practice should precede theory; that experience is the best way to learn about color; and that trial and error are valuable teachers.

In accordance with this approach, students in the workshop were presented with colored paper and problems to solve. Under the guidance of a professor from the Yale University School of Art, we experimented with our colored papers, putting together different combinations of hues. Some of the optical illusions were surprising indeed. But in the unstable, ever-changing world of the garden, these same optical illusions are almost impossible to re-create.

After all the colored papers, all the reading, and all the questions to my eye doctor about color vision, I eventually found myself pretty much back where I started. Right along, I believed that a gardener's best bet was to study the color wheel and to learn the way the children at the museum were learning—by looking at paintings.

I felt that it was important to pay close attention to the relationships and degrees of likeness and difference between colors and to understand the principles of contrast and harmony. Once you have grasped the rudiments of these two techniques, you have it made.

With nature providing an abundance of soft, neutral tones and peace-keeping green leaves, no gardener with keen eyes can go that far wrong. And at the risk of oversimplifying a complex subject, I still maintain that color for gardeners isn't so complicated after all.